In praise of *Red Scare in the Green Mountains*

"Gracefully written, full of wonderful, well-chosen details.... Focusing on the witch hunt era in one state, with just enough national background to put the stories in context, Winston depicts the politics of demagoguery and resistance—a topic that couldn't be more timely for all Americans today."

> – Marjorie Heins, author of *Priests of Our Democracy:*
> *The Supreme Court, Academic Freedom, and the*
> *Anti-Communist Purge*

"...sheds a new light on a dark chapter in American history. We are introduced to leaders who deserve their place in history, such as Congressman William Meyer and Professor Andrew Nuquist...a well-researched picture of Vermont in the McCarthy era"

> – Madeleine Kunin, former Vermont governor,
> author of *The New Feminist Agenda*

"Rick Winston has written a highly informative book that expanded my knowledge of Vermont during the 1950s and during the McCarthy years. It is well-written and immediately drew me in. I recommend the book to all those interested in the Vermont experience, McCarthyism, or our efforts to protect our rights in challenging times."

> – Gregory Sanford, former Vermont State Archivist

"...shines a penetrating light on and compellingly recreates the little-known story of how valiant Vermonters rallied to withstand the pressures and distortions of the McCarthy Era. Strikingly relevant for our own era."

> – Tony Hiss, author of *The View from Alger's Window*

"...an important story about how hate and fear preached by national figures impacts people living in small towns across America. To understand how a demagogue can lie, scapegoat and bully his way to power, it is enlightening to revisit how residents and leaders of the small state of Vermont both collaborated with and fiercely resisted the anti-communist witch hunts of Sen. Joseph McCarthy."

> – David Goodman, author and host,
> *The Vermont Conversation*

"…a fascinating exploration of the way McCarthyism and related right-wing fear-mongering played out in a state that is commonly thought of as uncommonly liberal. The reality… is that intolerance, xenophobia and fear of 'un-American' ideas are ugly stains on the history of all America—even in the state that produced Bernie Sanders."

> – Mark Potok, expert on the radical right and former
> Senior Fellow of the Southern Poverty Law Center

"*Red Scare in the Green Mountains* is quite compelling and establishes the story, with its now barely known opponents, and supporters, of McCarthyism, as one to read today. For the nasty, life-tearing, reputation-ruining, anti-commie campaign of 70 years ago has many similarities to what we're being swept along in with the Trump administration. As I'm sure some of Winston's characters thought or said, This can't happen here, it can. And will, if the momentum that the Republicans nationwide are now riding like power-drunk horsemen of the apocalypse is not brought to a halt."

> – Joe Sherman, author of *Fast Lane on a Dirt Road*

"A fascinating and highly readable history that shines a light on how Vermont wrestled with one of the most important American political episodes of the 20th century. …reveals the remarkable intersections of Vermont and national politics as each influenced the other in the spiraling rise and precipitous fall of McCarthyism.…shatters the illusion of a bucolic state immune to the Red Scare and offers important lessons for our times."

> – Prof. Woden Teachout, author of *Capture the Flag:*
> *A Political History of American Patriotism*

"Rick Winston's inspiring text takes us back to the dark days of the downward turn of American politics toward repression and persecution, but also of extreme bravery of many of New England's best, under terrible political pressure. Anyone interested in the effects of the McCarthy Era and its opponents will find an alarming but also moving saga here."

> – Paul Buhle, co-editor, *Encyclopedia of the*
> *American Left,* and author of *Marxism in the*
> *United States*

Red Scare
in the Green Mountains

Red Scare in the Green Mountains

Vermont in the McCarthy Era 1946–1960

RICK WINSTON

Rootstock Publishing

First Printing: July 25, 2018

ISBN-10: 1-57869-007-2
ISBN-13: 978-1-57869-007-7
Library of Congress Control Number: 2018934830

Rootstock 🍃 Publishing

Published by Rootstock Publishing an imprint of Multicultural Media, Inc.
www.rootstockpublishing.com
info@rootstockpublishing.com

"'A Sinister Poison:' the Red Scare Comes to Bethel" originally appeared in *Vermont History,* and is reprinted with the permission of the Vermont Historical Society; "The Vermont Press and Joseph McCarthy's Downfall" originally appeared in the *Walloomsack Review,* and is reprinted with the permission of the Bennington Museum.

Email the author at winsrick@sover.net for interviews and readings

Art and Book Design: Mason Singer, Laughing Bear Associates
Author photo by Jeb Wallace-Brodeur

Printed in the USA

To my parents,
Julia Kaufman Winston
and Leon Winston

Contents

Leon and Julia Winston, circa 1935

Preface

REFLECTIONS OF A
"RED DIAPER BABY"

The origins of this book date back to a conference held in Montpelier in 1988, "Vermont in the McCarthy Era." I was one of three organizers of the event, along with Michael Sherman, then director of the Vermont Historical Society, and the late Richard Hathaway, professor of history at Vermont College. Looking back over the list of panelists, I see that the conference happened just in time; William Hinton, Robert Mitchell, Martha Kennedy, Rabbi Max Wall, and Arnold Schein are among those who have died since then.

As stimulating as the conference proved to be, I never lost the sense that we had only scratched the surface. The intention of this book is to both explore some subjects that were not covered at the conference and also to give a greater shape to our findings.

As for the origins of my own interest in this topic, that has everything to do with my own parents' experiences during the Red Scare. My parents, both children of Eastern European immigrants, came of political age during the turbulent Depression years.

Like many Jews of their background, they found a place for their idealism and union activity (in their case, the New York City Teachers' Union) in the Communist Party. Then, as the political climate changed, they were, as Philip Roth put it, "impaled suddenly on their moment in time, caught in the trap set to ruin so many promising careers of that American era."

If there were such a thing as a typical childhood spent in the shadow of the Red Scare, mine was one. There were Paul Robeson

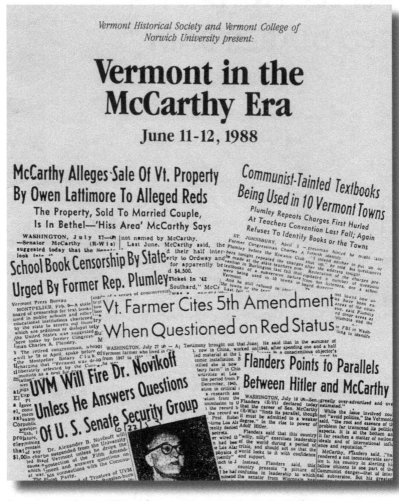

Program cover for the 1988 conference "Vermont in the McCarthy Era"

and Pete Seeger 78's; a very secular Jewish atmosphere; a left-leaning summer camp; a subscription to the left-wing *National Guardian* ("But don't tell anyone we get it!"); my feeling of isolation in a very conventional high school; and dinner-table correctives to what I had learned in history class that day.

However, every family that was chilled by the fear of the era had its own particular drama. I knew the basic outlines of my parents' stories, but not until I read their files from the New York City Board of Education archives a few years ago could I finally fill in certain gaps, more than fifty years after the fact.

When I first became curious about the Red Scare era and asked my parents how they were affected, they painted a vivid picture of the times and mentioned various family friends who had been teachers but were now working in other professions, such as insurance and electric repair. They were uncharacteristically reticent about themselves, keeping their own stories to a concise scenario.

My father's story involved a favorite student at Taft High School in the Bronx during the 1940s. That student was Harvey Matusow, who later became Joseph McCarthy's paid informant. "I knew my goose was cooked," said my father, "when Harvey named me at a HUAC hearing in Washington."

My mother's version went like this: "They finally got around to calling me before a New York City committee when the worst was over. I told them that I'd share anything about myself, but I wouldn't name anyone else."

In 2011, my parents' brief narratives were fleshed out when I received those files from the Board of Education archives— 22 pages in my father's case, over 60 in my mother's.

There in my father's file is the testimony of Matusow, in February of 1952: "In 1945, the correspondence to me from Mr. Winston expressed condemnation of the foreign and domestic policies of the Truman administration and generally supported the Soviet policy in connection with foreign affairs.... In the early part of 1947, I solicited Mr. Winston for funds in support of the American Youth for Democracy. He declined to contribute funds on the grounds that he had already pledged himself to supply funds directly to the Communist Party." I can just hear my father's voice commenting sarcastically, "A likely story."

In June of 1952, a letter appeared summoning my father to an interview with the Board of Education's own "Grand Inquisitor," Saul Moskoff, followed shortly by a letter dated September 1952, accepting his resignation. A family friend, apolitical himself but nevertheless disgusted by what he observed, offered to help my father start an art supplies store in the Cross County Shopping Center, then under construction near our home in Yonkers. I still have the edition of the Taft High School paper announcing his leaving school to go into private business, ending with the quote, "I'm going to miss the kids."

The letters from erstwhile colleagues (and former comrades) naming my parents as Communist Party members do not show up in their files until December 1954 and April 1955. My father used to say, "When the dust settled, you looked around and saw who was still teaching, and you had a pretty good idea of who gave names."

My mother's "invitation" to an interview with Saul Moskoff was issued in December 1955, and her testimony, running to 35 pages, was taken in January 1956. After warning her that refusal to give names might result in her dismissal (an appeal to end this policy was at that time pending before the Commissioner of Education), Moskoff finally (on page 28) put the question to her. She replied, "There's only one position I can take, and that is, I just couldn't. It would be against my principles, my scruples, I wouldn't be able to rest as easily as I do now, and live with myself as honestly as I do now."

Reading her testimony evoked yet more questions: Was she coached? Was it her own idea to emphasize her activities as a parent, an artist, and a participant in the community who really didn't have much time or mental energy for politics? Was her testimony given meekly, to throw her questioners off the scent, or defiantly, as I am certain she must have felt? Unfortunately, there are no stage directions in these pages.

Her story had a favorable outcome. She was able to keep her job at Washington Irving High School, and then spent the last fifteen years of her teaching career at Music and Art High School.

My father's outcome was a good one, too, after a fashion. He became a successful retailer, and seemed to be satisfied with this life. Late in his life, he answered most of my questions about the Red Scare era, but I never did ask him about the loss of the thing he was most passionate about—teaching art and design.

I heard someone say recently that although the blacklist claimed many victims, forcing them from their livelihoods, not many people talk about our own loss as a culture. There were films that were never made, songs that were never written, laughs that an audience never got to experience—and in my father's case, generations of students whose lives were never changed by someone who cared intensely about passing on his knowledge and creativity.

Today, in 2018, as our country finds itself facing new blacklists, fierce attacks on a free press, a revitalized white supremacy movement, and a political atmosphere charged with intolerance, condemnation, and widespread falsehoods, this book could not be timelier. We are in another era marked by fear and demagoguery, one in which the language of the Red Scare need only be modified slightly to fit today's perceived threats. We have a president who is quick to use the words "McCarthyism" and "witch hunt," but who himself uses the weapons deployed by the "witch-hunters." To make the historical circle complete, new stories of the last year tell us that Donald Trump's mentor in public life was the odious Roy Cohn, Joseph McCarthy's indispensable aide.

Vermont, more than many other states, avoided the worst effects of the Red Scare. My hope is that illuminating this period in our past will help us both understand the historical forces at work today and give us the inspiration to survive and thrive in treacherous times.

– Rick Winston
Adamant, Vermont

Richard O. Hathaway at the 1988 conference "Vermont in the McCarthy Era,"
with panelist Martha Kennedy. (Courtesy of the Vermont Historical Society)

Overview

THE RISE OF McCARTHY AND HIS "ISM"

By Richard O. Hathaway

The late and very much missed Richard O. Hathaway was one of the organizers of the 1988 conference, "Vermont in the McCarthy Era," presented by Vermont College and the Vermont Historical Society. The VHS recently summed up Dick's contributions well: "Richard Hathaway was a serious scholar, and he was at the same time a delightful, light-hearted man with a real understanding of Vermont history and genuine sympathy for the underdog. As teacher and historian, Richard Hathaway opened doors to the past and in doing so enlightened the present. Hundreds of students were grateful recipients of his gift as an exuberant and witty lecturer and his encyclopedic knowledge of American history." The historical overview that he wrote for the 1988 program guide still stands as a concise guide to the issues that will be discussed in this book. – Author's note

After 1945, American citizens pondered the shifts in power relations that marked the problematic aftermath of the Second World War. The Soviet Union was soon perceived as our foremost adversary rather than our unflinching wartime ally; Winston Churchill spoke of an Iron Curtain descending across Eastern Europe; Czechoslovakia became an obvious satellite of the Soviet Union in the distracted spring of 1948. One year later we were startled to learn that Russia possessed the A-Bomb, and that we had also allegedly "lost" China. The assault by North Korea on South

Korea in June, 1950 seemed to underline our worst fears that the times were out of joint, and that it was communists at home and abroad who, in a vast and efficient conspiracy, were subverting the planet as we had known it.

Senator Joseph McCarthy has become an icon of the shifting nature of this post-war world. His image suggests in its complexity the repercussions from the early Cold War, the anticommunist crusade, and the preoccupations with loyalty and subversion that continue to reverberate nearly forty years after these events transpired.

There are perhaps as many explanations of Joseph McCarthy and McCarthyism as there are commentators on this man and the movement he represents. To some, he expressed legitimate concern over unpatriotic, subversive figures who threatened the American way of life. To others he represented a populist impulse that aimed to cleanse our nation of "foreign" elements. To still others, McCarthy was a demagogue and a manipulative self-seeker interested in nothing so much as the last headline he had created with his speculative and unfounded charges against citizens whose main "crime" had been advocacy of highly unpopular points of view. Early scholarly interpretations treated McCarthyism as an aspect of "status anxiety," a by-product of the disruptions of modern life. Others viewed the movement as part of a conservative, capitalist effort to eliminate all views hostile to the prosecution of the growing Cold War between the U.S. and the U.S.S.R. Some viewed the man and movement as nurtured by a specious conservatism tinged with paranoia, in contrast to the more authentic conservatism of, say, Senators Ralph Flanders of Vermont and Arthur V. Watkins of Utah.

As historian Ellen Schrecker has convincingly stated in her recent work *No Ivory Tower: McCarthyism and the Universities,* McCarthyism was hurtful in spite of its relatively nonviolent character: "McCarthyism was amazingly effective. It produced one of the most severe episodes of political repression that the United States ever experienced. It was a peculiarly American style of repression—nonviolent and consensual." After all, she notes, the repression was mild, albeit efficient. Two were killed; a few hundred were incarcerated. While the blacklist deprived many of preferred

RUSSIA HAS ATOMIC BOMB!

U. S. Learns of Recent Explosion, President Discloses

Pentagon Shows Excitement, But Officials Mum

M'Carthy Charges Reds Hold U.S. Jobs

Cold War headlines: from the Davenport, Iowa *Democrat and Leader,*
September 29, 1949; from the Wheeling, West Virginia *Wheeling
Intelligencer,* February 9, 1950.

livelihoods for years, even decades, most were able to survive and
some even prospered, after a fashion.

Nevertheless, the price was high. Every section of society was
involved. A public agency identified those deemed subversive and
disloyal; the private sector then determined, after varying degrees
of due process, the nature of the punishment. This isolation and
hounding of the left in American politics resulted, at the least, in
a marked constriction of political debate for years after—some
would claim to the present time. Other scholars assert that our later
misadventures in Asia resulted, in part, from just that muffling of
dialogue and debate that followed our so-called loss of China in the late
forties, and the anti-communist impulses of the tormented fifties.

As we explore the McCarthy era in Vermont, at least two cau-
tions are in order. First, Senator McCarthy was not the originator
of the Cold War's anti-communist crusade. After all, several years
before McCarthy's allegations about cardcarrying communists in
the U.S. government, President Harry Truman and Congress had
fashioned through executive orders, supplementary legislation,
and relentless investigations a highly developed structure of loyalty
oaths and tests for alleged subversives.

Revisionist historian Richard M. Freeland has declared in his
The Truman Doctrine and the Origins of McCarthyism that Truman

had vigorously and deliberately exaggerated the intransigence of the Soviet Union and the dangers posed to our system by international and domestic communism, in order to mobilize the U.S. behind his foreign and trade policies of 1947–48. Thus, "the practices of McCarthyism were Truman's practices in cruder hands, just as the language of McCarthyism was Truman's language, in less well-meaning voices." The emotions and patterns of belief of the "Cold War consensus" were essentially developed by early 1948. McCarthy, then, was merely one of the most energetic—some would say reckless—in exploiting a system already in place.

The second caution: it has long been the case, when viewing the McCarthy era in Vermont, to stress the differences between Vermont and neighboring New Hampshire in their manifestations of McCarthyism. The standard version declares that New Hampshire witnessed persistent assaults on civil liberties by both individuals and the state's governmental apparatus. Conversely, the Vermont scene was allegedly marked by only occasional forays by marginal figures, with Vermont's record manifesting respect for individual liberties, and a lack of anti-communist hysteria and witch-hunting. These comparisons are partly true, but gloss over important exceptions to the rule of respect for civil liberties in the Green Mountain state.

To be sure, Senator Flanders ultimately became a leading force in moving to strip Senator McCarthy of his powers as Chair of the Senate Committee on Government Operations, and led the fight to censure McCarthy in the summer and fall of 1954. But in 1953, after a painful and protracted process, the University of Vermont had stripped Professor Alex B. Novikoff of his faculty post for his "crime" of invoking the Fifth Amendment before the U.S. Senate Judiciary Committee. This episode was perhaps the most significant demonstration of McCarthyism in Vermont. But other figures, such as former congressman Charles A. Plumley, declared that subversive textbooks were being used in at least ten Vermont towns, and that the state was a "testing ground for the Communists." Other studies have suggested that Senator McCarthy was held in deep regard by many Vermonters in the early fifties.

Perhaps our relatively microscopic exploration of "history through a blade of grass" will suggest perspectives that a telescopic view alone cannot provide. After all, we have yet to comprehend fully the legacy of McCarthy and McCarthyism. We must continue to define state and national practices that sustain both national security and liberty for our citizens.

Political cartoonist "Herblock "(Herbert Block) is generally credited with coining the term "McCarthyism." Cartoon from April 1950. (Courtesy of The Herbert Block Foundation)

The cover of a 1947 comic book published by the Catechetical Guild Educational Society

THE RED SCARE ERA IN VERMONT AND ELSEWHERE: A TIMELINE

1934

Charles Plumley of Northfield wins first term as congressman

1935

Founding of Putney School

1941

William Loeb III buys the *St. Albans Messenger*; Vilhjalmur Stefansson buys property in Bethel

1942

William Loeb III buys the *Burlington Daily News*

1945

Yalta and Potsdam Conferences; end of World War II

1946

Andrew E. Nuquist challenges Charles Plumley in the Republican primary for Vermont's congressional seat

1946

Winston Churchill introduces the phrase "iron curtain'" in a Fulton, Missouri, speech: "From Stettin in the Baltic to Trieste in the Adriatic an 'iron curtain' has descended across the continent."

1947

President Truman signs Executive Order 9835, establishing the Loyalty Program

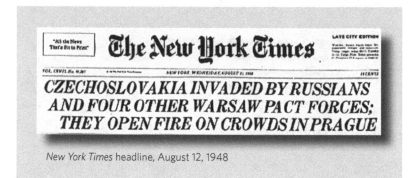

New York Times headline, August 12, 1948

1948

March: Communist-led government formed in Czechoslovakia

April: Marshall Plan announced, giving major economic aid to Europe

June: Berlin airlift, one of the first major crises of the Cold War

1948

January: Henry Wallace announces Progressive Party candidacy for president

February: Vermont Wallace for President Committee formed

March: Dean Luther McNair forced to resign at Lyndon State Teachers College as a result of pro-Wallace activity

May: Rockwell Kent speaks at the University of Vermont supporting Wallace

August: Alger Hiss accused of being a Soviet spy

1949

July: Owen Lattimore buys land in Bethel

October: Mao Zedong officially proclaims the establishment of the People's Republic of China, naming himself as head of state; Zhou Enlai is named premier

November: Bernard and Sheila O'Shea buy the *Swanton Courier*

1950

January: Alger Hiss convicted of perjury

February: In a speech in Wheeling, West Virginia, Joseph McCarthy claims there are 205 "card-carrying" communists in the State Department

March: McCarthy names Lattimore as "top spy" in the State Department

June: Lattimore sells land to Ordway and Mary Southard, inspiring McCarthy's charge that "Reds infest Vermont"

June: Start of Korean War

August: Indictment of Julius and Ethel Rosenberg on espionage charges

September: At the Vermont State Republican convention, Charles Plumley insists communists are using Vermonters as "guinea pigs"

New York Daily News headline, June 26, 1950

1951

In his inaugural address, Governor Lee Emerson calls on the legislature to update the Sabotage Prevention Act "to make it applicable under present day conditions"

1952–1955

Lucille and Manuel Miller publish *Green Mountain Rifleman* newsletter

1952

New Hampshire General Court passes Subversive Activities Act

1953

March: Death of Joseph Stalin

March: Plumley-inspired textbook censorship bill defeated in Vermont House

April: Alex Novikoff of University of Vermont refuses to name colleagues at a Senate investigation; in September he is fired from the university

June: Execution of Julius and Ethel Rosenberg

August: William Hinton returns from China; his notes are confiscated by the U.S. Customs Agency

1954

Geneva Accords divide Vietnam

1954

January: Paul Sweezy and Gwynne Harris Daggett testify before New Hampshire attorney general Louis Wyman

April: Army-McCarthy hearings begin

July: Senator Ralph Flanders introduces Senate motion to censure Joseph McCarthy

July: William Hinton testifies before U.S. Senate Internal Security Committee

December: McCarthy censured by 67-22 vote in U.S. Senate

1956

Soviets quash Hungarian uprising

1958

William H. Meyer becomes the first Democrat in Vermont to win a congressional seat in 104 years

1959

January: Success of Cuban Revolution led by Fidel Castro

December: Rev. Willard Uphaus begins New Hampshire jail term for refusing to turn over World Fellowship Center records

1960

Meyer loses bid for re-election to Robert Stafford

1966

William Hinton's *Fanshen* published

Whom Does Plumley Represent?

The State of Vermont has only **one** Representative in the House at Washington. This is a big responsibility for Vermont's Representative —only **one** man in the House to speak for all Vermont! Mr. Charles A. Plumley has been Vermont's **only** Representative in the House of Representatives for 12 years. What kind of a job has Plumley done? **Whom does he represent?**

The Farmer?

Labor?

The Veteran?

The Consumer?   Business?

DOES PLUMLEY REPRESENT THE VERMONT FARMER?

No! He voted against extending the operations of the Electric Home and Farm Authority. Is the Vermont farmer not to have the benefits of rural electrification, Mr. Plumley? He voted against the Disaster Loan Corporation. Where and when has Mr. Plumley supported the interests of the Vermont farmer in Congress? **Mr. Plumley does not represent the farmers of Vermont.**

DOES PLUMLEY REPRESENT THE VERMONT CONSUMER?

No! He voted for every crippling amendment to the price control program. Is the Vermont consumer to have no protection against soaring rents and prices, Mr. Plumley? **Mr. Plumley does not represent the consumers of Vermont.**

DOES PLUMLEY REPRESENT VERMONT BUSINESS AND LABOR?

No! Mr. Plumley voted for the Case Bill, for the amendment to the Hobbs Bill. This is not the spirit of Vermont industrial relations, Mr. Plumley! Vermont is famous for its peaceful, constructive labor-management relations. Would you destroy this by restrictive legislation, Mr. Plumley? Mr. Plumley voted against the Full Employment Bill. Are Vermont business and Vermont labor to have no protection against depression? Where and when has Mr. Plumley supported the interests of Vermont business and Vermont labor in Congress? **Mr. Plumley does not represent the employers and workers of Vermont.**

DOES PLUMLEY REPRESENT THE VERMONT VETERAN?

No! He voted against giving the National Housing Authority sufficient funds to operate. **Where is the veteran going to live, Mr. Plumley?**

Our Senators Are Respected!

Vermont's Senators have earned the respect of the entire nation. Senator Aiken and Senator Austin are among the ablest leaders of the Senate. Let's carry this record into the House! Vermont's **one** Representative should truly represent Vermont—the Vermont farmer, the Vermont consumer, Vermont business and Vermont labor.

VERMONT FAVORS A FAR-SIGHTED FOREIGN POLICY

For years the citizens of Vermont have led the nation in pressing for a far-sighted foreign policy. Our Vermont Senators—Senator Aiken and Senator Austin—have played distinguished parts in Congress in building a peaceful world. What about Representative Plumley? He voted **against** extension of Selective Service, **against** extension of the Reciprocal Trade Agreements Act to promote U. S. foreign trade, for crippling amendments to the United Nations Relief and Rehabilitation Administration. Is this the way the United States is to meet its international obligations, Mr. Plumley? Is this the way you represent the voters of Vermont?

MR. PLUMLEY'S ABSENTEEISM

Besides, much of the time, Mr. Plumley does not vote at all! In fact, much of the time he is nowhere near the House of Representatives! Is this the way Vermont is to be represented in Congress?

CHAPTER ONE / 1946

THE CONGRESSMAN AND THE PROFESSOR

As long as there have been "Reds," there has been "Red-baiting," which is the tendency to associate dissenting beliefs with communism, socialism, or anarchism. The term took hold during what historians call "the first Red Scare," the period following the Russian Revolution when left-leaning political activists in the United States were jailed or, like Emma Goldman, deported. A fear of communist subversion or indoctrination was a feature of the American political landscape long before Senator Joseph McCarthy emerged in February 1950 and loaned the "second Red Scare" his name.

From 1934 to 1950, Vermont's lone congressman was Charles Plumley of Northfield. He was known for "his red-baiting and anti-labor speeches," according to a *Life* magazine spread in the fall of 1942 on potential new members of Congress, including Plumley's primary opponent, Sam Ogden. As the campaign progressed, Plumley accused Ogden, a Landgrove architect and writer, of having leftist tendencies. Plumley won the election by a two-to-one margin.

When a University of Vermont political science professor, Andrew E. Nuquist, challenged Plumley four years later in the 1946 Republican primary, it wasn't long before author and poet Walter Hard wrote in the *Rutland Herald:*

> Of our Congressman's consistency,
> This much can be said.
> Whoever runs against him
> He's sure to find out he's a Red.

"Old Charlie must know his time is up"

Charles Plumley was one of Northfield's most celebrated natives. He served in the Vermont legislature for two terms, was president of Norwich University from 1920 to 1934, and then was Vermont's Republican congressman until 1951. But outside Northfield, Plumley

Congressman Charles Plumley of Northfield, Vermont

Nuquist Attacks Plumley's Absence At House Sessions

Burlington Free Press, August 9, 1946

was better known for his role as Vermont's premier anti-communist crusader. If Vermont had its own version of Senator McCarthy, it would have been "Uncle Charlie," as he was popularly known. The nickname was used with affection by his supporters and with disdain by his detractors.

Plumley had joined the anti-communist bandwagon as early as 1940, when he became a vocal opponent of history textbooks written by Harold O. Rugg, a follower of educational theorist John Dewey. Rugg's history textbooks cast a critical eye on certain aspects of American society (such as a recognition of economic inequality and a characterization of the founding fathers as landed gentry). The textbooks became the target of a national campaign, led by the Hearst newspaper chain. Plumley tried, but failed, to have the books removed from Vermont classrooms.

As *Life* magazine had pointed out, Plumley also had a long history of opposing organized labor, associating it with communists at every opportunity. "I believe that the greatest danger to responsible organized labor comes not from outside its ranks but from those who, filled with Communist teachings are forever boring from within," he said on one occasion. "And some of the latter already have vantage points of power."[1]

------

[1] Dorothy Canfield Fisher, an ardent free speech defender, quoted a neighbor in *Vermont Traditions* (1953): "Anyone who tries to bore from within in Vermont is going to strike granite."

Facing only token Democratic opposition in each general election, Plumley was re-elected easily term after term. But his lackadaisical performance in Congress and his increasingly erratic behavior, including public inebriation, worried many Republicans. As editor John Hooper stated in the *Brattleboro Reformer* in 1946, "Old Charlie must know that his time is up.... He has displeased Old Guard leaders as much as he has harried labor leaders."

Plumley's record of anti-labor votes was one of the issues that led a forty-year-old professor of political science, Andrew E. Nuquist, to challenge Plumley for the Republican nomination in 1946. Nuquist, from a small town in rural Nebraska, had relocated to Vermont in 1938 after completing his doctorate at the University of Wisconsin. As his daughter Elizabeth Raby remembered, "When my father arrived in Vermont, his field of interest was international relations. Very soon, however, he became fascinated by his adopted state. Although he always retained his internationalist outlook, he became a specialist in the local and state governments of Vermont." During his tenure as associate professor of political science at the University of Vermont, Nuquist served on many civic and war-related bodies: he was chair of the Vermont State Chamber of Commerce Committee on Local Finances and Affairs from 1941 to 1943, a public panel member of the Regional War Labor Board from 1943 to 1946, and director of the Town Officers' Educational Conference in 1946.

Elizabeth Raby set the scene in her memoir *Ransomed Voices:*

My father has been approached by a group of prominent men who think it is well past time for a change. "I can't afford a campaign," my father tells them. "How much do you need?" they ask. "Five thousand dollars," he answers, and it has been provided. My mother gives up her position as president of the Burlington League of Women Voters to manage my father's campaign. She has no experience running a campaign, but my father has long depended upon her organizational skills. My father worries that he is still considered a newcomer to the state, a flatlander, having lived in Vermont for only eight years, and he has the misfortune of teaching at the university. He's heard that people think he's Jewish because of his thin beak of a nose and his strange name.

Andrew Nuquist's campaign literature. Note slogan "Sober Consideration of All Legislation" (courtesy of University of Vermont Special Collections)

Nuquist's official campaign announcement began, "The changing times and pressing postwar problems require the careful and full attention of a young, vigorous and trained representative." He believed he was qualified because of his "extensive study of the procedures of government, because of his interest in local government, and his unshakeable belief in representative government as the foundation of the American way of life."

Several editorial writers could not hide their excitement that "Uncle Charlie" might have a formidable opponent. "A certain Vermont professor is said to be angling for a nomination to Congress," wrote one. "To the labor and farm group, the professor has shown himself to be a man who will champion their interests. The picture of Vermont Republicans nominating a left-winger is difficult to see, but a farm-labor raid on the Republican primary might put the professor across."

Another of Plumley's detractors in the press put it this way: "There are Vermonters who like Uncle Charlie's act. And that's one of the things that makes Vermont so much more interesting than the 'quaint' sort of state it has been billed as for far too long on the outside. There is considerably more variety than quaintness in the people who inhabit the Green Mountains, a variety that ranges from the reactionary Charlie Plumley to the liberal Andrew Nuquist."

Nuquist staked out a position in favor of the Saint Lawrence Seaway (a pet project of Senator George Aiken's, opposed by Plumley) and called attention to Plumley's votes against the United Nations Relief and Rehabilitation Administration ("essential as a basis of promoting world peace") and the Rural Electrification Administration ("Congressman Plumley appeared before a REA hearing and stated that the reason Vermont farmers lack electrical energy is because they don't want it"). Noting Plumley's minimal participation in Congress, Nuquist said, "This is not the kind of representation that Vermont should have...in these days of vital change and world-shaping events, we need leadership. I am awake to the obstacles in the way of world peace, and enough of an idealist to believe that something can be done to ensure peace."

The *Rutland Herald* noted Nuquist's animated campaign: "Not satisfied with a token campaign, Nuquist has been covering the state carefully and energetically, making many friends and some votes in addition to the usual fixed opposition to Rep. Plumley.... He has shown ability at campaigning which indicates that he knows something more than the theory of politics."

What criticism was expressed that spring was aimed at Nuquist's newcomer status, the depth of his Republican convictions (he had supported Roosevelt in 1944), and his intellectual leanings.

Citing his graduation from the "left-wing dominated University of Wisconsin," Rockwood Publications, owner of several Addison County newspapers, claimed, "This youthful professor in the science of politics would foist upon us theories of socialism— mildewed debris of intellectual fancy."

A controversial meeting in Barre

But late that June, Nuquist's plans to challenge Plumley's congressional record ran into a more serious roadblock in the form of a purported endorsement from a small group of communists in Barre, as reported in the *Barre Times*. Under the headline "Communists Meet," the news story covered a meeting at which "about 25 local Communists" heard Hy Gordon, a Communist Party organizer from Massachusetts, speak on the subject "Is World War III Inevitable?" During the course of the meeting, "Thomas Cerasoli, head of the local party, asked the audience to support Prof. Walter [sic] Nuquist in his campaign" and referred to Nuquist being "cooperative to written appeals from the Party."

The original article appeared on April 30, 1946, but the news did not spread until late June, when it was seized upon by the archconservative editor of the Essex Junction *Suburban List,* Milo Reynolds: "It is very evident that the Communists would not be urged to support Nuquist unless they knew what they might expect from him were he nominated and elected. From this fact, there can hardly be any stronger argument given for support to Charles A. Plumley for Congress."

Reynolds' editorial was noted by other pro-Plumley newspapers, including the *Bennington Banner* and the *Caledonian Record.* An editorial in the *Bellows Falls Times* stated, "We talked with a man who knew him [Nuquist] vaguely and classed him as a 'pink.' That has been a serious trouble with the Nuquist campaign from the beginning, the undercurrent with the 'red' complexion. The fact is Plumley has gained strength by voting for laws that would curb some of the power that unionized labor is tossing around irresponsibly."

Andrew Nuquist Again Denies Communist Charge

ARGUS 8-8-46

RUTLAND, Aug. 8—Andrew E. Nuquist, Congressional candidate in the Republican primaries Tuesday, last night challenged Rep. Charles A. Plumley "to prove a single one of his charges that I am in any way connected with or sympathetic with the ideas or actions of the Communists" in a radio address here.

"The simple truth of the matter is that he is not able to substantiate his charges and is not willing to try to do so publicly," Nuquist asserted.

"I want to state here and now that I am not, have not been and never intend to be a Communist. I do not like the ideas, tactics or programs of the Communists, either in this country, in Russia or in any other nation."

Nuquist said that "the program of Rep. Charles A. Plumley is a technique used by persons who have no arguments in their own behalf against their opponents. It is an outworn method of appealing to the emotions of their audience and not to their intellects."

"It is easy to smear a person with the term 'red' because it cannot be defined or even fully explained. It is a method used to the fullest by men like Rankin of Mississippi or Talmadge of Georgia and has its effects in those backward areas.

"I do not believe that the program can be effective here in Vermont. This Communist smear is a desperate effort to try to put the campaign on the level of the gutter and is really an insult to the intelligence of the voters of Vermont and should be so considered by them.

Montpelier Argus, August 8, 1946

Nuquist on the defensive

Soon Nuquist publicly challenged Reynolds. He wrote to the *Suburban List* and circulated the letter to other newspapers: "I am hurt that when I go about improving a bad situation in Washington, I find that because I have some civic pride I am labeled with such a term of opprobrium.... You should have known that a man in my position whose work is to know government policies and philosophies would not be likely to go contrary to the principles of free government... it does both me and the citizens of this area a disservice which is fraught with danger." Challenging the accuracy of the original article, Nuquist added, "It seems rather poor judgment to take the word of the *Barre Times* in this matter when all you had to do to correct the misconception was to pick up the telephone and call me."

The *Bennington Banner,* under the editorship of Ralph "Ginger" Howe, took an additional swipe after receiving Nuquist's letter: "Every patriotic Vermonter would be foolish to replace Plumley with someone whose practical experience in life has been small and in a narrow circle.... We never heard of Mr. Nuquist until he became a candidate with ambition to force one of Vermont's most valuable citizens back into private life."

Nuquist's angry reply to this letter is tantalizing in what he hints at, but never quite says: "I am also shocked to read your statements about Mr. Plumley and his usefulness in Washington. I cannot believe you are so uninformed or naïve not to know the stories that are current in all these parts of the state as to his actions in Washington, or to be ignorant of the stories told about him in Washington, as well as reports of the actions witnessed by scores of citizens of this state who are ashamed to have him as their representative."[2]

The communist issue dogged Nuquist through the rest of the campaign. From headlines such as "Plumley's Opponent Declares

------

[2] Nuquist's son, Andrew S. Nuquist, notes that it was no accident that his father's campaign slogan was "Sober consideration of all legislation." "This may not be a very revealing slogan to some," said the *Newport Express,* "but to many it will mean even more than the words indicate."

Charles A. Plumley: Vermont in Danger

Duane Lockard was a longtime professor of politics at Princeton University. The first of his several books was New England State Politics, *published in 1961. Here he writes about the last act of Charles Plumley's anti-communist crusade.*

In 1953 Charles A. Plumley, a 77-year-old veteran of eighteen years in the United States House of Representatives, apparently decided that Vermont was in danger. Perhaps he was unhappy in his political retirement and wanted some excitement; for whatever reason, he urged that Vermont censor her school textbooks to cull out those of subversive nature. Accordingly, a neighbor of Plumley's introduced a bill into the Vermont House of Representatives to implement the former Congressman's ideas. The bill called for an appointed board to survey all textbooks and to withdraw any that had "subversive or disloyal" content (neither of these terms being defined).

Plumley had several texts in mind that he wanted exorcised. He contended that Vermont was a "testing ground for the Communists," citing as an item of evidence that Alger Hiss had a home in the little town of Peacham. Late in March a move was started to get Plumley to address a joint session of the General Assembly, but several leaders blocked this, one calling it "an effort at back-door lobbying." The newspapers failed to take up the cry and demand censorship; most of them were critical of the bill. The teachers were opposed, and there was considerable popular opposition to the bill as an invasion of the powers of locally elected school boards. Yet the same kind of opposition to such legislation had been heard in many other states where it became law. Teacher opposition, the desire for local autonomy, and the uncertainties of such vaguely worded law having failed to halt censorship elsewhere, many Vermont-

House Kills School Book Censorship Bill

Plumley-Supported Measure Slapped Down 202-11

Burlington Free Press, March 31, 1953

ers thought the bill might pass. The Appropriations Committee of the House ended the speculation in late March when it voted fourteen to one against the bill. (The Education Committee had passed it on to Appropriations without recommendation.) The House itself made it final when only eleven affirmative votes could be mustered against the 202 "nays." The House turned a deaf ear to Plumley's warning of danger as well as to his plea that a similar law had worked well in New York. The reporting member of the Appropriations Committee said they would not put "the stamp of approval on $1,000 for this witch hunt."

Vt. Educators Challenge Plumley To Name Reds Teaching in State

Burlington Free Press, October 6, 1950

Assembly Rebuffs Plumley, Cancels His Talk On Reds

Vermont Press Bureau

MONTPELIER, March 10 — Former Congressman Charles A. Plumley suffered a rebuff in the Legislature today, leading to cancellation of his scheduled address on Vermont Communist activity and textbook censorship in schools.

The appearance of Plumley before a joint assembly blew up when the Senate refused to hear him before 9 p.m. and Plumley refused to begin his speech any later than 8:15 p.m. He was scheduled to speak tonight.

Hours before Rep. Pernice V. Bromley of Weathersfield withdrew a resolution providing for the joint House - Senate assembly, there were clear signs of antagonism toward a second appearance of the 77 - year-old ex - congressman before the legislature.

Burlington Free Press, October 6, 1950

Plumley Urges Probe of Reds In Vt. Schools

Congressman Tells GOP Some Textbooks Are Communistic

Morning Press Bureau

MONTPELIER, Sept. 29 — Rep. Charles A. Plumley, addressing the GCP state convention here today, called for the investigation and removal of Communists, fellow travelers and sympathizers and their influence from the state's schools and colleges.

He said the call for leadership by the Republican party has never been so loud and compelling, that while time has been lost, at least we are awake, "It is not too late if Republicans organize effectively to meet the challenge of tyranny," he said.

"Chosen As Guinea Pigs"

Declaring that Vermont had been deliberately selected by the Communists for a testing ground, Rep. Plumley said, "Nobody doubts that Vermont was selected and that Vermonters were chosen as a bunch of guinea pigs on which to

Burlington Free Press, September 30, 1950

Monopolies Are Dangerous" and "Nuquist Gets Labor Backing," it was now "Nuquist Denies Communism Charge." At a campaign debate in Middlebury a week before the election, Plumley branded Nuquist as "coming from that hotbed of radicalism, the University of Wisconsin, to tell Vermonters how to run their own affairs."

Plumley received many newspaper endorsements, ranging from lukewarm ("Nuquist should be a bit better known before giving him a strong endorsement") to enthusiastic, while Nuquist got nods from very few papers, among them the *Springfield Reporter,* the *Swanton Courier,* and the *White River Valley Herald.* Nuquist did get the full support of the Vermont branch of the labor confederation Congress of Industrial Organizations (CIO); the CIO president, Raymond Jenkins, noted that "not once has Plumley voted for labor." Plumley wasted no time in using this endorsement as proof that Nuquist had communist leanings.

Nuquist took an early lead on election night, but when the votes were counted, he had won only his home base, Chittenden County, losing statewide by 8,000 votes. Although Plumley kept up his Red charges to the end, Nuquist did not blame the communist issue for his defeat. He told his daughter Elizabeth, "I didn't have time to get to everyplace.... I lost where they didn't have a chance to hear me. If I'd gotten into the thing sooner, I might have pulled it off. But I'm still an outsider here." His son, Andrew S. Nuquist, recalls his father admitting he never thought he had much of a chance, but felt that someone had to show it was possible to wage a strong anti-Plumley campaign.

In 1948, when Nuquist's name was brought up as a possible challenger again, the *Rutland Herald* stated that "Nuquist had nothing to recommend him as a candidate two years ago when he started out. But he turned out to be an exceptionally good campaigner.... . With a greater background of experience and acquaintance in Vermont legislative and political circles, he would probably have defeated Plumley." But Nuquist decided that once was enough. His moderate success in 1946, however, led to four Republican candidates challenging Plumley in 1948. Plumley won easily for what turned out to be his final term.

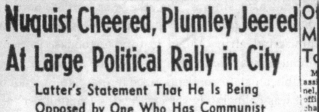

Nuquist Cheered, Plumley Jeered At Large Political Rally in City

Latter's Statement That He Is Being Opposed by One Who Has Communist Endorsement Proves Quite Unpopular

Burlington Free Press, August 9, 1946

Plumley Charges CIO With Breaking Law in Campaign Ads

NORTHFIELD, Aug. 11.— Congressman Plumley tonight charged the CIO with open violation of federal law in their political activities directed against his re-election and in their activities in the interest of Professor Nuquist.

Plumley, in his statement, said: "The left-wing members of the CIO have not been content with their campaign of vilification and misrepresentation against me and their active support of my opponent. They have now openly violated federal law in this campaign by their sponsorship of anonymous, quarter-page political advertisements filled with misstatement of fact, which recently appeared in not one but several newspapers of the Vermont press, and by their sponsorship of these unsigned, unidentified advertisement they have not only rendered themselves liable to federal prosecution but have seriously involved the newspapers carrying their misleading and anonymous advertisments as well.

"The seriousness of the offense is made clearly evident by the penalty provided for the violation. The law provides a fine of up to $1000 or imprisonment for not more than one year or both.

"This last exhibit of the professor's campaign against my re-election should confirm all that I have said concerning the type of campaign being conducted against me by him. He has attempted to disallow the Communist endorsement given him. I wonder how he will try to talk himself out of this predicament."

The federal law cited, Plumley stated, is 18 U. S. C. A. 62-62B.

Rutland Herald, August 12, 1946

"Stay home, Mr. Plumley"

Plumley had two separate swan songs. One was in 1950, as he was finishing out his last term. The other was in 1953. Both involved attempts to once again urge Vermont to recognize the danger of communist indoctrination in history textbooks. In September 1950, months away from his retirement, he delivered a speech to the Republican state convention, charging, "No one doubts that Vermont was deliberately selected by the Communists as a nest for experimentation." This proposal met with strong opposition from both the education commissioner, A. John Holden, and the representative assembly of the Vermont Education Association, which unanimously challenged the congressman to produce evidence of communism in Vermont or withdraw his statement ("No comment," said Plumley).

In 1953, Plumley's Northfield neighbor, Charles Barber, introduced Plumley-inspired legislation to set up a school textbook censorship board. Save for William Loeb's *Burlington Daily News* and *St. Albans Messenger,* Vermont newspapers were adamantly opposed to the proposed legislation. Gerald McLaughlin of the *Springfield Reporter* said, "We think there's enough character assassination going on in Washington under the guise of Red hunting without extending it into our Vermont schools....This sort of thing, if permitted to run hog wild, could result soon in boards of censorship on all phases of our life. And we don't think Vermonters like that." Robert Mitchell of the *Rutland Herald* added, "The proposal may be one of those flag-waving, hurrah-boys measures which is politically difficult to oppose. But we hope not."

Plumley had hoped to address a joint session of the Vermont legislature on the issue of the communist threat, but he was rebuffed. Stan MacPherson, writing in the Capital City column in the *Swanton Courier,* thought that "former congressman Charles Plumley probably isn't too fond of the state senate these days after that body blocked his address before a joint session last week. Senators Corliss of Windsor and Howe of Bennington decided the address didn't warrant a joint session and succeeded in changing the time of the address, which was a polite way for the Senate to say, 'Stay home, Mr. Plumley.'" The defeat of the textbook bill ended Plumley's public career. Other states had their own "mini-McCarthys": John Tenney in California, Philip Bowker in Massachusetts, Albert F. Canwell of Washington, and Louis Wyman in New Hampshire. But after Plumley's retirement, there was no Vermont political figure who took on that role.

Andrew Nuquist was never again tempted to run for political office. He continued his teaching at the University of Vermont, where he remained until he retired in 1970. Along with his teaching duties, he served as executive director of the League of Cities and Towns for two years, president of the Vermont Children's Aid Society for six, and member of the Vermont Legislative Reapportionment Board for eight. He authored two books on local government in Vermont (the second co-authored with his wife, Edith), and in 1982, seven years after his death, an annual undergraduate award was established by the university's Center for Research on Vermont in his name. By the time the *Vermont Encyclopedia* was published in 2003, it was Nuquist and not Plumley who received an entry.

Portrait of Henry Wallace by master caricaturist David Levine
(copyright Matthew and Eva Levine)

CHAPTER TWO / 1948

THE HENRY WALLACE CAMPAIGN IN VERMONT

Two years before Senator Joseph McCarthy burst onto the national scene, Vermont experienced its first major manifestation of that potent mix of super-patriotism, staunch anti-communism, and fear tactics that characterized the Red Scare era. The occasion was the quixotic presidential campaign of Henry Wallace in 1948, when Wallace mounted a third-party challenge to both incumbent Democratic president Harry Truman and his Republican rival, New York governor Thomas E. Dewey.

Bernie Sanders' presidential run in 2106 drew comparisons with that 1948 campaign, bringing the hazily remembered figure of Henry Agard Wallace back into public view. Wallace had been a person of international renown at the close of World War II, ranking in a June 1946 poll as one of those "most admired" in the United States. But by the time the Vermont chapter of the Wallace for President campaign was formed in February 1948, he had become marginalized and, in some quarters, reviled for his political positions.

Out of step in the postwar world

He had been an inspiring and accomplished Secretary of Agriculture during the hardest years of the Depression and served as President Franklin Roosevelt's vice president from 1940 to 1944. For many, Wallace was the person most closely associated with Roosevelt's New Deal next to Roosevelt himself. Wallace embodied New Deal political values with his wartime advocacy of "the century of the common man," based on pro-labor and anti-monopoly policies at home and U.S.–Soviet cooperation abroad. He was a strong advocate for a national health program and an outspoken supporter of civil rights.

Roosevelt had appointed Wallace Secretary of Commerce during his fourth term, but after Roosevelt's death and the collapse of the U.S.–USSR wartime alliance, Wallace feuded with both the new president, Harry Truman, and Truman's anti-Soviet Secretary of State, James Byrnes. Truman fired Wallace from the Commerce post in September 1946, freeing Wallace to voice ever more provocative opinions about the growing Cold War conflict. As Ira Katznelson wrote in *Fear Itself,* a history of the Roosevelt years published in 2013: "While others saw ominous signs in Soviet speech and behavior, Wallace's vocal minority focused on the fact that the Soviets had taken positions that were not unreasonable about German reparations, reconstruction of Italy and Japan, and other strategic issues."

Wallace became editor of the influential left-leaning *New Republic* magazine, which provided a platform for him to criticize Truman's foreign policy. By the time he announced his presidential candidacy on the Progressive Party ticket in 1948, he was viewed by many as someone out of step with the post–World War II world. The platform of the Progressive Party (or the New Party, as it was called in some quarters) advocated friendly relations with the Soviet Union, an end to the nascent Cold War, an end to racial segregation, and universal government health insurance.

The *New Yorker* writer Alex Ross commented in a 2013 article, "Wallace's messianic belief in his abilities to single-handedly reverse US foreign policy led him into treacherous waters."

The Communist Party, along with the militant union federation, the Congress of Industrial Organizations, served as Wallace's grassroots organizing force, leaving his campaign open to strong criticism from both Republicans and establishment Democrats. The launch of Wallace's presidential campaign in February 1948 suffered from particularly poor timing, coming as it did in the same month as the Soviet coup in Czechoslovakia and the suspicious suicide (years later, proven to be murder) of the Czech leader Jan Masaryk.

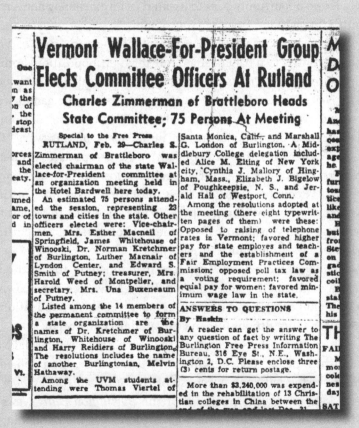

Burlington Free Press, March 1, 1948

The suggestion in those days that the United States and the Soviet Union were equally to blame for Cold War hostilities was hard enough for many Americans to swallow. But to maintain, as Wallace and some supporters did, that the fault was mainly if not all on the American side was far beyond the accepted parameters of discussion. As Curtis MacDougall writes in *Gideon's Army,* a voluminous history of the Wallace campaign, "there was hardly another state in which the New Party was taken more seriously—as a menace—than in the Green Mountain State. Instead of welcoming the movement as an aid to Republicans, the press of the state let no opportunity pass to assail it as an extremely dangerous Leftish threat to the American way of life."

Although no newspapers in Vermont were in favor of Wallace's platform, two papers stood out for their opposition, both in Burlington: the *Burlington Free Press* and, above all, the *Burlington Daily News.* The editorials from these papers ran the gamut from sneering disdain to apoplectic outrage. Historian David Holmes characterizes the two Burlington newspapers in this way: "The *Daily News* conveyed a virulent right-wing perspective, while the *Free Press* assumed an editorial position close to the Eisenhower brand of Republicanism." Holmes observes, "The first instinct of most of Vermont's newspapers at this time was to accept the messages from Washington about the state of world affairs, particularly about the Communist threat."

The *Burlington Free Press* is still publishing today, though greatly diminished; the *Burlington Daily News,* the paper owned by William Loeb III, is a distant memory. It ceased publication in 1959 after a tumultuous fifteen years under Loeb's reign.

Although most people associate Loeb with his influential New Hampshire paper, the *Manchester Union-Leader*, his publishing career started with the purchase of the *St. Albans Messenger* in 1942, followed by the purchase of the *Burlington Daily News* in 1944. One of Loeb's early infamous exploits was the publishing of his own baptismal certificate on the front page of both Vermont papers in an attempt to disprove rumors of his Jewish ancestry. He bought the *Manchester Union-Leader* in 1948, and it was there he gained the national reputation as a publisher many politicians dared not cross.

As *Daily News* publisher, Loeb occasionally used his front page for signed editorials, often with a strident right-wing message. Shortly after Wallace announced his candidacy, the *Daily News* called Wallace "America's Rabble Rouser #1," blasting his refusal to condemn the Soviet Union for the February 1948 takeover of Czechoslovakia. Under the headline "Our American Fuhrer," the editorial stated, "His strange ideology had seemed to be the product of half-baked thinking, a dreamy-eyed prophesying unworthy of serious examination." Loeb continued, "But that can no longer be true. While his utterances here at home are dangerously close to outright sedition against our own nation, he could not more loyally serve the Kremlin by his passionate attacks on capitalism and his unashamed support of many things Communistic."

The attack on Luther Macnair

The first newsworthy incident of the Wallace campaign in Vermont occurred shortly after the formation of the state organizing committee in February. In late March 1948, Luther Macnair, a dean at Lyndon Teachers College, addressed a Wallace for President meeting in Burlington. Recalling the late Wendell Willkie's description of the "reservoir of good will" the United States had throughout the world and his warning that it was diminishing, Macnair argued that the recent history of U.S. foreign policy was further threatening that reservoir.

"American strength is not being thrown on the side of people struggling for freedom," he insisted, and he classed American action in Indonesia, China, the Middle East, Turkey, Greece, and Spain as supporting elements of reaction in the world. "I covet for our country the role of supporting all people struggling for freedom," noted Macnair, "but instead we see ourselves on the side of reactionary forces everywhere."

During a question session, Macnair declared he saw no reason to consider the Soviet Union aggressive. He explained the coup in

EDITORIAL

MacNair Should Go

Today our nation is dangerously close to a new war. If this next war starts according to the trend of world affairs at this critical moment, we will again be engaged in a war that is not of our own making.

Our enemy will be Soviet Russia, and the war will come as a direct result of her plans to rule the world.

There is no escaping these conclusions. The proof has been offered in countless ways, the Red scheme of aggression being patterned closely along the same lines followed by Adolf Hitler.

This then is the horrible threat hanging over our heads today—the threat that Stalin and his killers may force us to go to war to stop the Russian enslavement of many nations.

When we know these facts, and they are now self-evident, it is outrageous to learn that no less a person than a history teacher of the Lyndon State Teachers College is going around the state preaching a doctrine strongly defending the Communists in their program of world expansion.

This individual, Vice-Principal Luther MacNair, has a perfect right to support Henry Wallace if he wishes. He also has a perfect right to indulge privately in the belief that Russia's program can be understood, that Wallace is really for peace and freedom, and that the nations which oppose Russia are "reactionist" and "fascist."

Vice-Principal MacNair made these assertions in a talk before a Wallace rally in Burlington last Friday evening. He even went to the extreme of defending the Red rape of

(Continued on Page Two)

Burlington Free Press, March 22, 1948

Czechoslovakia as provoked by reactionary forces, and he raised other points that were anathema to the *Burlington Daily News,* which responded with a front-page editorial declaring "Macnair Should Go": "It is outrageous to learn that no less a person than a history teacher of the Lyndon State Teachers College is going around the state preaching a doctrine strongly defending the Communists in their program of world expansion." The *Free Press* weighed in as well: "Dean Macnair's frank following of the Communist line is serious because he is in a position to influence public thinking…. If he is ignorant of the fact of Soviet aggression, is he a competent leader in the field of education? If he knows it, what shall we say of his honesty?"

But it was the *Daily News* that kept up a barrage of criticism during that week. Macnair did not publicly defend his remarks and did not respond to the *Burlington Daily News'* campaign. Although the *Free Press* published both anti- and pro-Macnair letters, including a letter of support signed by five former students, William Loeb's paper did not have a letters section. Before the week was out, Macnair had submitted his resignation.

A *Daily News* article of March 28, headlined "Macnair Resigned in Time to Escape State School Board Inquiry," made clear that the newspaper was taking credit for keeping the controversy on full boil; Loeb had brought the state board of education into the picture by personally sending Commissioner Ralph E. Noble a copy of Macnair's speech. Whether such an investigation into Macnair's teaching was actually planned or simply after-the-fact public relations is unknown. The *Daily News* took the opportunity for one last strongly worded "good riddance" editorial titled "Sing On, Macnair, Sing On": "Dr. Noble and the state board are to be commended for their promptness in becoming aware of the situation," stated the editorial. "Mr. Macnair has long been known as an extreme left-wing radical; his ideological display at the Wallace rally clearly indicated that his rabid personal opinions were based on distorted ideas rather than on truth." Macnair then disappeared from the news. The entire controversy spanned just a week and a half.[1]

- - - - - -

[1] After resigning from Lyndon State, Macnair and his family moved to Cambridge, Massachusetts, where his ailing father lived. After working at various odd jobs, in 1950 he became executive director of the Massachusetts chapter of the American Civil Liberties Union, a post he held until 1970. He died in 1988 at age eighty-three, and the Massachusetts ACLU now gives an annual award in his name. When I contacted that group a few years ago to find out more about Macnair, I was stunned to learn that his widow, Louise, aged 107, was still alive. She has since died, at age 109, but I was able to see her in Cambridge and ask some questions about the 1948 controversy. What she was able to remember was that her husband thought highly of the president of Lyndon State at the time, Rita Bole, and resigned to spare her and the college unwanted attention.

James Hayford:
Recalling the Wallace Convention

James Hayford was a poet, educator, musician, and political activist. In addition to publishing several volumes of poetry, he wrote a fascinating memoir, Recollecting Who I Was. *In it, he recounts his experience at the Progressive Party convention in July 1948, when Henry Wallace was nominated for president.*

Progressive Party convention, July, 1948

I helped draw up the state platform at the Vermont convention for our "New Party," at Brattleboro, and was elected a delegate to the national founding convention in Philadelphia, July 23–25, 1948. I took the train to New York, where Bill Sweets put me up overnight. In Philadelphia I roomed with Frank Gentile, Universalist minister from St. Johnsbury.

Frank and I read copies of the proposed platform: plank after plank condemned United States foreign policy. Not that we wholly disagreed, in most instances, but the implication was that our policy was all wrong while the Soviet policy was all right. This rubbed Frank and me the wrong way. In the first place we didn't believe this was true. In the second place, the press had been predicting that Wallace would allow his Communist allies to dominate the thinking of the convention; this kind of platform would support the charge. A mischievous thought occurred to Frank, and I guess to me at the same moment: a resolution putting the convention on record as not giving blanket approval to the foreign policy of any nation would a) satisfy those of us who were disinclined to blame Washington for ALL the world's ills, b) demonstrate that our Communist friends were not dictating to the convention, and thus c) give us a defense, however slight, against some of the Red-baiting we knew we were all going to be subjected to in campaigning for Wallace and the "Progressive Party," as we soon voted to call ourselves.

What we didn't know was that the same thought had occurred to certain members of the Platform Committee, especially to Professor Frederick L. Schuman of Williams College, who had presented an addition to the "American-Soviet Agreement" section of the platform, which read, in part:

"Responsibility for this tragic prospect (threat of another war) is an American responsibility insofar as the leaders of the bipartisan foreign policy have placed monopolistic profits and military power ahead of peace in the dealings with other nations. It is a Soviet responsibility insofar as the leaders of the Soviet Union have subordinated the preservation of peace and concord to aggrandizement and power politics..."

The Platform Committee debated this addition to such great length before accepting it that it arrived at the printers too late to be included into the copies of the platform we had seen.

Frank and I worked out the language of what was to become known as the "Vermont Resolution," and, since Frank was hoarse from cheering at the rally in Shibe Park the night before, I rose and introduced it. We had tried to get the concurrence of the whole Vermont delegation, but only Helen MacMartin of Burlington went along with us.

Back in Vermont I found I was regarded with even more suspicion than I had been before the convention. The Vermont press reasoned that the defeat of our resolution had proved beyond any doubt that the convention was Communist-controlled. One out-of-state Communist called on me in West Burke to ask contemptuously how much I been paid by capitalists to split the convention.

One thing I was, was impossibly thin-skinned, too thin-skinned for a career in politics.

Sharing a joke at expense of "reactionary forces," their popular term for Republican and Democratic party leaders, Wallace followers laugh off Communist leanings alleged against their new party a few hours before Artist Rockwell Kent (left above) said in a speech here that he thanked God for the Communist support of Wallace. Pictured at cocktail party before Kent's address here last night are Kent, Dr. Norman Kretchner, UVM Medical College research director and state Wallace worker, and Mrs. Helen MacMartin, chairman of local Wallace group and state director of the third party.—(Daily News Staff Photo—Campbell.)

Rockwell Kent Welcomes Aid For Wallace from Commies

(Special to The Daily News)   us. What fools we would be to attending were members of the

Rockwell Kent (left) is welcomed to Burlington. *Burlington Free Press*, 1948.

"Kent's charm is disgusting"

The next major controversy to arise during the Wallace campaign was the Burlington appearance of Rockwell Kent on May 20. Kent was an American painter, printmaker, illustrator, and writer who had been a nationally known figure in the arts dating from the 1920s. As World War II approached, Kent shifted his priorities, becoming increasingly active in left-wing politics and increasingly supportive of Soviet-American friendship and a world devoid of nuclear weapons. In 1938 the U.S. Post Office asked him to paint a mural in its headquarters in Washington, D.C. The mural depicted mail delivery in Puerto Rico, and Kent included a postcard from Alaska with a message (in Inuit dialect and in tiny letters) that read when translated, "To the people of Puerto Rico, our friends! Go ahead. Let us change chiefs. That alone can make us free!"

Kent's identity as an American painter receded in the postwar years; the more he spoke out on world issues, the more he became, along with other prominent intellectuals and creative artists, a target of anti-communists. At the time of his appearance in Burlington, he had been embroiled in controversy in his hometown of Ausable Forks, New York. His successful dairy business had been boycotted due to his political views, specifically his support of Wallace. One resident was quoted as saying, "We refuse to buy Russian milk." In a story that appeared in the Burlington newspapers on the very same day in March as Luther Macnair's resignation, Kent canceled his insurance and other business ties, signing over the farm to two of his workers there.

Kent was the guest speaker at a University of Vermont Students for Wallace meeting that May. Perhaps feeling that he had nothing to lose, he delivered an incendiary speech, prompting the headline in the next day's *Burlington Daily News,* "Rockwell Kent Welcomes Aid for Wallace from Commies." "God bless the Communists for their support of Henry Wallace," said Kent in Burlington. "They have offered their aid to us. What fools we would be to refuse them." He went on, "It is true that Wallace has the support of the Communists, and also true that Republicans and Democrats have the support of every crook and gangster in the country."[2]

The Daily News also editorialized about the speech, with the headline "Kent's Charm Is Disgusting." The paper called the speech "a collection of frustrated opinions parading as facts, a parcel of lies gathered with care to create disrespect for our government and

------

[2] During the 1950s, Kent received several invitations to attend international conferences, but was denied a passport. In 1958, he was the plaintiff in Kent v. Dulles, 357 U.S. 116, a major Supreme Court case vindicating the constitutional right to travel and invalidating the government's denial of a passport to Kent based on his political beliefs.

support for Henry Wallace and the Communists." It went on, "No good citizen should distort the truth by saying—without any factual proof whatever—that ours is a government 'of corporations, by corporations, and for corporations.'" The editorial concluded, "The visit of Mr. Kent to Burlington was a good thing for one reason only: it gave good Americans a chance to see just how far wrong an idealistic guy can go when he indulges in an emotional orgy supporting such a demagogue as Henry Wallace."

"The Wallace Breeze" in Burlington

By the time candidate Wallace made an appearance in Burlington in June 1948, it was apparent that his presidential campaign was in trouble, both nationally and statewide. Inexperience and lack of organization led to difficulty in selling tickets to Wallace's Memorial Auditorium rally. In addition, many people were clearly reluctant to be associated with the campaign; Curtis MacDougall reports in *Gideon's Army* that it took many phone calls to find a farmer willing to allow a noon picnic lunch on his property and it took fourteen calls to obtain an accompanist for Bob Penn, one of the stars of the Broadway musical *Oklahoma,* who was slated to sing at the rally.

By this time, the tone of the *Free Press* and *Daily News* editorials had moved from outright alarm into condescending dismissal. A few days before Wallace's personal appearance, the *Daily News* editorialized, with prescience as it happened: "He is being very naïve, indeed, if he expects to pick up many supporters hereabouts. Henry, a persistent fellow if ever there was one, said his third-party group would take away votes from both Republicans and Democrats. We have a sneaking suspicion that Henry should be getting ready, about now, for an awful surprise."

Describing Wallace's sparsely attended speech at Memorial Auditorium, the *Free Press* mocked his campaign slogan of bringing "a fresh breeze to American politics" and stated, "The kindest explanation of Wallace the candidate is that much learning has made him mad. The Wallace breeze, we are sorry to say, seems

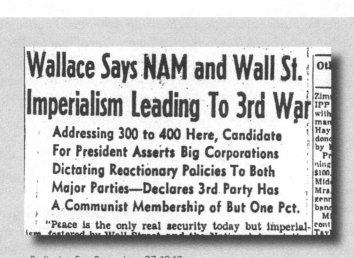

Burlington Free Press, June 27, 1948

like a zephyr that has become balmy." However, this bemused attitude did not prevent the *Free Press* from publishing the names of everyone at the rally who gave money, with their identifying towns and the donation amounts. "Several Well-Known Persons Give Checks of $100 or More" read a headline. Among those "well-known persons" were two state officers of the Wallace campaign, Charles Zimmerman of Brattleboro and Una Buxenbaum of Putney; two professors, Lucien Hanks of Bennington College and Waldo Heinrichs of Middlebury; and Rockwell Kent.

The *Daily News* also treated Wallace's speech with bemused condescension: "During his appearance in Burlington this weekend, Henry Wallace impressed observers as a rather pathetic figure, a man who has been misdirected in his efforts, probably sincere, to gain world peace." That editorial also pointed out that "however sincere he may be, his tie-in with Communists, whether direct or indirect, will be his final undoing."

In this, William Loeb was correct, for as Wallace biographers John Culver and John Hyde write: "Each new chapter in the Red Scare only further isolated Wallace and his party.... By the time of the election, his credibility as a political figure was destroyed and his party removed to the fringe of public life."

The Vermont delegation to the Progressive Party convention played an unexpected role in the further erosion of that credibility. James Hayford, a farmer and poet, was a strong Wallace supporter who attended the Progressive Party convention in July 1948, yet was leery of the pro-Soviet slant of many Wallace supporters. Together with delegate Frank Gentile of St. Johnsbury, Hayford crafted what became known as the "Vermont Resolution," which read, "Although we are critical of the present foreign policy of the United States, it is not our intention to give blanket endorsement to the foreign policy of any nation."

The famed journalist H.L. Mencken described what happened next: "When an honest but humorless Yankee tried to get in a plank disclaiming any intention to support Russian assassins in any eventuality, it was first given a hard parliamentary squeeze by the Moscow fuglemen on the platform, and then bawled to death on the floor." As Hayford wrote in his memoir, "Back in Vermont I was regarded with even more suspicion than I had been before the convention. The Vermont press reasoned that the defeat of our resolution had proven beyond any doubt that the convention was Communist-controlled."

The Vermont Progressive Party soldiered on, holding a state convention in Brattleboro in early October. Its platform included abolishing farm taxes, bolstering workers' compensation funds, creating a fair employment practices law, establishing farmer-consumer cooperatives, and developing a Connecticut Valley Authority modeled on the Tennessee Valley Authority. These proposals were not mentioned in the *Brattleboro Reformer* editorial the next day; instead, the paper admonished the Progressives for being "another drum corps in Henry Wallace's parade" and for not fielding any statewide candidates.

A month later, on Election Day, the national tally for Wallace was just over one million votes and a fourth-place finish behind South Carolina senator Strom Thurmond and the segregationist States' Rights Party. In a development that must have been especially dispiriting to Vermont supporters, Wallace fared worse in Vermont than he did nationally, garnering 1,679 votes for only 1.04 percent of the total count.

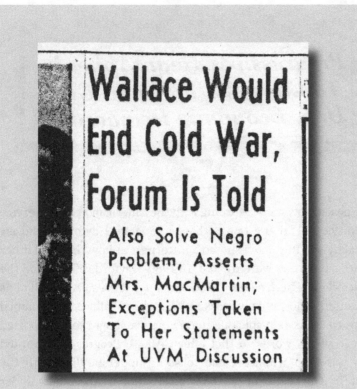

Wallace Would End Cold War, Forum Is Told

Also Solve Negro Problem, Asserts Mrs. MacMartin; Exceptions Taken To Her Statements At UVM Discussion

Burlington Free Press, August 4, 1948

After the election, an embittered and disillusioned Wallace pulled back from party-building efforts. As he watched his position in Washington sink from respect to derision, he began to recant his attachment to left-wing politics, drawing further away from hard-line ideologues and adding criticism of the USSR to his speeches. The Progressive Party's opposition to American involvement in the Korean War precipitated a final break, and in 1950 he left the party that he had helped to found.

In Vermont, the Progressive Party maintained a presence through the 1952 presidential election, largely due to untiring efforts by Helen McMartin of Burlington (the chair of the 1948 Vermonters for Wallace Committee), and then withered away. Some Progressive Party stalwarts like McMartin and Martha Kennedy remained active in the peace movement, working with the American Friends Service Committee and other groups; others, like James Hayford, withdrew from activism. But many shared a bitterness at how they and other Wallace supporters were treated. In 1989, Hayford reflected on the Wallace campaign in a letter to the *Burlington Free Press*: "All of us Vermonters who publicly worked for Henry Wallace were named in your columns as suspicious characters who ought to be deported to Moscow—or words to that effect. All we Progressives wanted to do was help Wallace come to some understanding with the Soviets.... Our platform called for international agreements under which both nations would be spared from living forever under the threat of sudden nuclear annihilation."

It was noted by some commentators in early 2016 that Bernie Sanders, like Wallace, was treated by the media and the Democratic Party establishment with a similar hostility and disdain. But Wallace, running a marginal campaign before the days of widespread television, never got the exposure that Sanders did. Alexander Heffner, one of many contemporary observers drawing the comparison between the two campaigns, noted, "In choosing to run as a Democrat, Sanders has clearly learned a lesson from Henry Wallace's unsuccessful 1948 third-party presidential campaign." Along with the many accomplishments of the Sanders campaign, a small but significant one might be that the figure of Henry Wallace and the story of the 1948 presidential campaign have enjoyed renewed attention.

The Wallace Breeze

Henry Wallace came to Burlington last Saturday. He saw the city and some of its citizens saw him, but there was no indication that he conquered very many. Some money was raised in his behalf (how much probably we shall never know), but it took considerable talking on the part of the financial expert of the party to get it. As a result of that and other preliminaries, Henry himself did not appear on the Memorial Auditorium platform until 10:20 p. m.

By that time, some had already departed the hall. Others looked as though they felt like it, and the candidate himself looked and acted weary, as well he might on a hot night after a busy day. Thus there was an unfortunate lack of the "fresh breeze" which some of the speakers said was blowing across the country for Wallace. Many hoped this much-publicized breeze would appear when Wallace began to speak, but it was a vain hope.

Wallace said the Republicans and Democrats are just alike—that they are both bad medicine for the country and that the only hope is to elect him President. He didn't explain how, in case a miracle should happen and he did get elected, he would assure peace to the world in spite of the activities of an unregenerate Congress made up of the bad Republicans and Democrats. The assumption is that he intends to abolish Congress by some political magic, though he didn't actually say so.

The kindest explanation of Henry Wallace, the candidate for President, is that much learning (he admits to speaking several languages and being a scientist, businessman, prophet and son of a prophet) has made him mad. The Wallace breeze, we are sorry to say, seems like a zephyr which has become a bit balmy. We hope this egomania does not prove fatal.

Burlingon Free Press, June 27, 1948

| 33 |

Rutland Herald, August 17, 1950

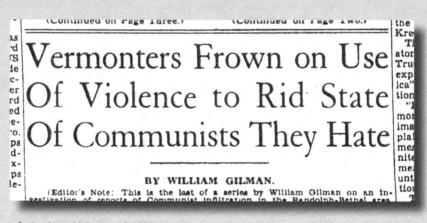

Rutland Herald, August 19, 1950

CHAPTER THREE / 1950

"A SINISTER POISON": THE RED SCARE COMES TO BETHEL

H ere's a question to stump many Vermont history buffs: Who was Ordway Mabson Southard? A May 2001 obituary for this prolific poet and haiku specialist noted some of the places he and his wife Mary had lived: Alaska, Mexico, Alabama, Hawaii, and British Columbia—but no mention of Vermont.

Yet it was here in the summer of 1950 that the Southards set off a chain of events that thrust Vermont into the national news. Only a passing obituary reference to their political activities ("Both were highly influenced by Marxist Socialist thought and participated in the Civil Rights Movement.") gives a clue to the incident that led to headlines such as one in the August 3 issue of the *Bradford Opinion*: "Reds Infest Bethel, Randolph Center, McCarthy Charges."

The events of that summer demonstrated Vermont was fully vulnerable to the national fear and suspicion that marked the period known as "the McCarthy Era." Two of the most public and persistent Vermont critics of this "Red Scare" were newspapermen, and each played a vital role in defusing that episode: Robert Mitchell, who had edited the *Rutland Herald* since 1941, and became its editor-publisher in 1948; and John Drysdale, who had published the *White River Valley Herald* and *Bradford Opinion* since 1945. In 1991, Drysdale was inducted into the Community Newspaper Hall of Fame with his citation noting his role discrediting claims that the Bethel-Randolph area was a "hotbed of communism."

Mitchell and Drysdale were among several major figures involved in the Bethel-Randolph controversy, which also featured a Tibetan Buddhist dignitary, a local self-described "Red hunter," and two well-traveled, prolific authors who, unlike Ordway Southard, were nationally prominent: the Far East expert Owen Lattimore, and the Arctic explorer Vilhjalmur Stefansson.

"Two exceptional men"

The story begins with Stefansson who first came to Bethel in 1941. By then he was a renowned veteran of several Arctic expeditions beginning in 1906 and later author of several landmark books about the Far North. He was born in Winnipeg to Icelandic immigrant parents, and grew up in rural North Dakota. While a student at Harvard Divinity School, Stefansson took a course in anthropology and soon transferred to that department. A Harvard mentor, Professor Frederic Putnam, convinced him to master the field without the trappings of academia, and Stefansson soon started his travels without having completed his degree.

The Icelandic author Haldor Laxness described Stefansson as "a poetry-loving academic, who gets up from his writing desk, wipes the ink off his fingers and becomes an Eskimo, in order to expand the boundaries of science to include the nations of the Arctic." During the 1920s and '30s he was based in New York City and amassed an extensive research library, open to students of the Arctic. Stefansson had difficulty adjusting to the sweltering summers of New York, and on the advice of his secretary, who summered in Gaysville, Vermont started looking for property in the state. Shortly after his marriage to Evelyn Baird in 1941, he bought "The Dearing Place," a farmhouse

Vilhjalmur and Evelyn Stefansson on their porch in Bethel, Vermont, 1948 (courtesy Dartmouth College Library)

and land in Bethel, a small town about 20 miles south of the state capital, Montpelier.

During their time in Bethel, which often was as long as five months of the year, the couple was active in the life of the town with Stefansson addressing various club meetings, and Evelyn singing in the church choir. After Stefansson learned that an adjoining property—known as "The Stoddard Place"—was to be logged, he convinced Charlie Andersen, the first mate on his expeditions, to buy it. But Andersen left after a few seasons and Stefansson bought the property. In 1947, he and Evelyn invited their good friends, Owen and Eleanor Lattimore, to stay for the summer, and during that time they made plans for the Stoddard Place to become a summer center for Asiatic studies.

Owen Lattimore was born in Washington, D.C. in 1900, but shortly afterward his father moved the family to Shanghai, China to take a teaching position. By the time the younger Lattimore was in his twenties, he had traveled widely in China and was a fluent

Chinese speaker. On his honeymoon in 1925, he and his wife Eleanor (who became his major collaborator) traveled across northern China and Mongolia, where he formed a deep connection with the Mongol people and empathy for their autonomy struggles. Among their close friends was a "Living Buddha" (somewhat akin to a cardinal of the Roman Catholic Church) known as Dilowa Hutukhtu, who would play a role in Lattimore's time in Vermont years later.

In 1937, Lattimore became a professor at Johns Hopkins University and by the start of World War II was widely regarded as one of the world's leading authorities on central Asia. In 1940, President Franklin D. Roosevelt chose him to be a personal emissary to Generalissimo Chiang Kai-Shek, a post he held until his appointment in 1942 to head the Pacific Operations of the Office of War Information. During this period he lectured, wrote, and edited *Pacific Affairs,* the influential magazine of the Institute for Pacific Relations.

Lattimore and Stefansson met at an annual meeting of the American Philosophical Society during Lattimore's first year at Johns Hopkins and quickly became close friends. Their wives bonded soon thereafter. Stefansson's wife Evelyn later recalled the special kind of dialogue that Owen and "Stef" had when conditions were right.

> These two exceptional men, each expert in his chosen field and interested in everything that related to it directly or peripherally, would begin [a conversation]. In comparing Eskimo and Mongol ways, no detail was too small to be recited and followed by evaluation, comparison, and speculation. Both brought marvelous but different linguistic accomplishments to the discussion. Each could stir the other intellectually and bring out his best. [1]

------

[1] Evelyn Nef was a fascinating woman in her own right. Born Evelyn Schwartz in Brooklyn NY, she was a cabaret singer and puppeteer in Greenwich Village in the 1930s. She and Stefansson were both regulars at Romany Marie's, a popular Village gathering spot. After an early marriage to puppeteer Bil Baird ended in divorce, she was asked by Stefansson to be an assistant at his personal library. They soon fell in love and despite their age difference of over 30 years, married in 1941. After Stefansson's death in 1962, she moved to Washington, DC, remarried, and, at age 60, became a psychotherapist. She died at age 96 in 2009.

Owen Lattimore in the Stefanssons' kitchen, 1949 (courtesy Dartmouth College Library)

In his memoir, *Discovery,* Stefansson describes "admiring [Lattimore] for the scholar that he was and liking him for his companionable geniality and friendly openness."

By the time these four friends developed the idea of the summer center in Bethel, the postwar political landscape was undergoing a severe change, with an increasing fear of communism and a suspicion of "heretical ideas" about foreign policy. The Federal Bureau of Investigation started files on both Stefansson and Lattimore long before Senator McCarthy came on the scene. In Lattimore's case, his support for the Maryland Civil Liberties Committee in 1941 was enough to get an FBI file started. As Ellen Schrecker, a leading historian of that era, has noted, "Had observers known in the 1950s what they have learned since the 1970s, when the Freedom of Information Act opened the Bureau's files, 'McCarthyism' would probably be called 'Hooverism,'" in reference to the longtime director of the FBI, J. Edgar Hoover.

In the 1940s, Stefansson, like many anthropologists, was already under FBI suspicion for the causes he supported. The fact that he was about to undertake his long-planned Encyclopedia Arctica with the active assistance of Soviet experts on the Arctic only heightened his profile. Stefansson's offer to the Boy Scouts to use his farm for Arctic camping lessons led to a sensational January 1948 article in the Hearst-controlled *New York Journal-American*. In that article he was identified as belonging to seventy-six different "Communist front" organizations, (such as the Committee for the Protection of the Foreign Born and Committee of Fair Play for Puerto Rico). The Boy Scouts consequently rejected his offer, "for the protection of the Boy Scouts of America from possible public criticism."[2]

Lattimore's FBI file had been deactivated during the war, but by 1949 previously discredited witnesses were getting a second hearing from the agency, and the file was reopened. As turmoil in China increased, Lattimore began speaking publicly about his disenchantment with Chiang Kai-Shek, urging American policy makers to adjust to the possibility of an eventual victory by Mao Zedong's communist insurgency, and arguing that Mao was not necessarily a pawn of Russian communists. His strong opinions, forcibly expressed, made him powerful enemies, especially those on the right looking for scapegoats for the "loss" of China to the communists.

In May 1949, both Lattimore and Stefansson appeared on a list of 102 speakers and entertainers judged by the American Legion's National Americanism Commission to be "unsuitable for Legion sponsorship." They were among only a handful of academics on a list that included Lena Horne, Paul Robeson, Lillian Hellman, Burl Ives, and Gene Kelly. Lattimore sent a letter to Stefansson asking,

------

[2]David Price, in his book *Threatening Anthropology* (Raleigh, NC: Duke University Press, 2004), argues convincingly that anthropologists, committed by the nature of their work to equality of the races, were more likely to be involved in anti-racist political groups than were other academics. Because the Communist Party was the most active organization fighting racism in the 1930s and 1940s, many other anti-racist groups were suspected by the FBI as being potentially subversive.

"What do you do about such newspaper stories, ignore them or write and demand to know on what grounds they make slurring remarks?" Unfortunately, there is no record of Stefansson's response.

That letter was one of many that spring between the two families as they considered the land purchase and the necessary renovations. Lattimore proposed bringing some Mongolian exiles and the Lattimores' son David enlisted some of his Harvard classmates to help with the renovations. The Lattimores wrote to Stefansson:

> We don't at present see ourselves spending many summers in Vermont and would like to know what you think of the prospects of renting, or selling within a few years. If you think of the present sale value as being about $1000 and we put $1600 into fixing it up it would have to sell for about $3000, wouldn't it, to cover taxes, agents fee, etc.?

Stefansson replied,
> The way local Vermonters now look at it...they put a lot of store by houses and barns, even if decrepit, and do not value hill land very much, if recently cut over, as ours is. They value meadows a bit more and there are I think about 30 acres of meadow in the 60 or 80 acre patch of land west of the road. But it seems to me for purposes of sale to city slickers, a good sized piece of land to go along with the house is important. So I suggest we consider, for investment purposes, joint ownership of the buildings and of the land that is west of the road.....

> The kudos of having been a Mongol citadel and having been built up by the Lattimores and a squad of Harvard sophomores should make the Stoddard place a conversation piece and easy to rent at a good figure whenever you do not want to use it for yourselves, family or friends....This letter is just thinking out loud. The main thing Ev and I want is that the deal shall go through. We want you at Dearing and the Mongols at Stoddard, and will do whatever to bring this about.

The arrival of the Mongolians, including Lattimore's old friend, Dilowa Hutukhtu, the "Living Buddha," was a source of excitement for the town of Bethel that summer. A front page article in the *White River Valley Herald* announced, "Buddhist High Dignitary Here for

Bradford D. Smith:
"A Sinister Poison" in Another Small Town

Bradford D. Smith was a well-known author of historical biographies for children, with subjects including Captain John Smith, Daniel Webster, and Stephen Decatur. He had been the wartime chief of the Central Pacific Office of War Information and the director of the Quaker International School in New Delhi, India. He and his wife, Marion, moved to southern Vermont in the early 1950s, and in this 1953 article for American Scholar *magazine, he describes how a warm welcome in his small town (Shaftsbury) turned to suspicion.*

Since we found acceptance so quickly, our shock was all the greater when friends from a distance called to see us one day. They had stopped at a store down the road to ask the way. "What do you think the owner said when we asked him if he knew Bradford Smith? He said, 'You mean that Communist?'"

Our friends thought it a great joke. WE didn't think it very funny, but we laughed too. Just at this time, [the conservative columnist] Westbrook Pegler had discovered that our state was full of Communists—most of them writers and artists, of course—so we attributed the shopkeeper's reaction to this much-publicized hogwash.

But a few days later, a friend from a nearby college stopped to ask if we would sign a petition being circulated by the Progressive Party. We said no, that we were not in sympathy with the Progressive Party and didn't want to be identified with it. "That's very funny," he said. "When I tried to get my filling station man to sign it, he said, 'I wouldn't sign anything that Bradford Smith was in.'"

A few days later, friends in a neighboring town asked us over for cocktails, saying that they wanted us to meet Mr. X. When we got there, we learned that Mr. X would not be present. "He said he was afraid your ideas would be too radical for him," they told us with a laugh.

Radical? I had not even taken an interest in party politics before the war, though residence abroad had given me an interest in international matters.

As a member of several college faculties, I had had a reputation for political conservatism.

Embarrassed that our hosts had lost a guest because of us, I said something about his peculiar behavior. "Oh, lots of people here think you're a Communist," they said, still laughing.

Only we weren't laughing any more. When we got home we tried to figure out how such a rumor had got started, but we couldn't. It was obvious now that we were surrounded by a large ring of suspicion of which we had been totally unaware, and that we were regarded as a source of contamination. By prodding our closest friends, we gradually learned the rumors being circulated:

I **must be a Communist because** I had no visible means of support, though my means of support was visible to anyone reading the Saturday Evening Post or the Reader's Digest.

I **must be a Communist because** in several public speeches I criticized the government for its wartime policies regarding internment of Japanese citizens.

I **must be a Communist because** I was going around the state (as a forum director) stirring up controversies about such things as socialized medicine and racial equality.

I **must be a Communist because** I was being investigated by the FBI (the investigation, I later learned, was undertaken because a government agency was about to invite me to take on a confidential job).

If I had been a self-employed shoemaker instead of a self-employed writer, they would probably not have fallen such ready victims to rumor, although why men who earn their livings with their minds are expected to be more vulnerable to intellectual frauds like communism, I have never understood.

What does it do to a man to find himself surrounded by suspicion, to know that though loyal and sensible friends will dismiss such idle rumormongering, the majority will conclude that where there is smoke there must be fire, that therefore he must be, at least partly, what rumor says? The worm of fear has gnawed its way deep into us all.

How true today?

Stefansson and Dilowa Hutukhtu; the "Dearing Place"
(courtesy Dartmouth College Library)

Summer on Bethel Farm," and reported, "The Dilowa was dressed in a long Chinese gown.... His bearing is very dignified and serene. He speaks no English except for a few simple phrases." An editorial on the following page noted, *"The White River Valley* is proud to welcome a Living Buddha.... We are sure that the dignified bearing of The Dilowa will be strengthened and fortified by his summer's communion with the Green Mountains." Longtime Bethel residents still remember the Dilowa's sweet tooth and his fondness for treating local youngsters to ice cream.

The daughter of another Mongolian visitor, Urgunge Onon, recently recalled, "Both my parents remember their time in Vermont fondly. Because of Owen Lattimore's great generosity, he took them (and me aged just 18 months) to Vermont to spend the summer in the old farmhouse. We were the first Mongolian family to go to Vermont."

A chill in the landscape

Neither Stefansson nor Lattimore was aware of the FBI's intense interest during the busy summer of 1949. The FBI took note of the Dilowa's presence and went as far as arranging the Bethel postmaster to intercept Lattimore's mail. That was the best they could do, since the isolation of the Stoddard and Dearing farms presented no easy cover for personal reconnaissance. The enthusiastic agent assigned to the case, A. Cornelius from the Albany, New York office, read mail, listened to phone recordings, and sent photographs of letters (some in Chinese and Mongol) to Washington for translation. Hundreds of copied letters to and from Lattimore ultimately wound up in bureau files.

Agent Cornelius also decided to read up on Buddhism, so that he could better understand what was taking place at the Stoddard farm. The theory he advanced was that Lattimore might be preparing the Dilowa to be the communist figurehead in Tibet. In fact, Lattimore was working diligently with his network of contacts in Asia to save rare Tibetan cultural manuscripts from the Chinese communists. As Lattimore had written that February to his friend

Luther Evans of the Library of Congress, "Tibet is clearly doomed to come under the control of the Chinese communists. There is, however, time for a planned salvage operation."

By late September, the Lattimores and their Mongolian friends were back in Baltimore. On September 18, Lattimore wrote to Stefansson, "We are already looking back nostalgically to the wonderful summer we had, and now Eleanor, as well as David and I, are looking forward to joining the deer hunting trip in November."

During the winter of 1949–50, further developments chilled the political landscape, most significantly the conviction in January of Alger Hiss on perjury charges. Hiss had denied being part of a secret Communist Party group in the State Department, and his conviction emboldened embittered ex-Communist informants like Louis Budenz, political enemies of Lattimore such as the wealthy importer Alfred Kohlberg, and unscrupulous politicians such as Senator Joseph McCarthy. In February 1950, McCarthy made his first major headlines when, in a speech in Wheeling, West Virginia, he claimed to have the names of 205 (variously stated as 57 and other numbers) Communists in the State Department.

Throughout February and March, McCarthy stayed in the headlines, promising to name the mastermind of this conspiracy. In March 1950, while Lattimore was on a United Nations–sponsored economic mission to Afghanistan, Senator McCarthy charged with great fanfare that Lattimore was in reality the highest-placed Soviet spy in the State Department. Despite McCarthy's haphazard methods (his charges took even the FBI by surprise), he had "a brilliant sense of timing and sure instinct for what an uncritical press and a disillusioned public would buy," according to Lattimore's biographer, Robert P. Newman.

Lattimore and his many supporters quickly dismissed McCarthy's charges as outlandish. Lattimore's telegram to the press, sent as he hastened home to face the charges, read in part, "McCarthy's off-record rantings moonshine.... Delighted his whole case rests on me as this means he will fall flat on his face." As Evelyn Stefansson Nef wrote in her memoir, "Could this be happening? In the United States? This felt like a Kafka novel in which unimaginable, terrifying nightmares occurred....Our scholarly friend Owen, the man who loved the Mongols and their culture as much as 'Stef' loved the Inuit—if it had not been so scary, it might almost have been funny." McCarthy quickly backpedaled when it came time to address the full Senate, downgrading Lattimore to someone who had "tremendous power in the State Department as the architect of Far Eastern policy." But the damage had been done to Lattimore's reputation.

It was easy to prove that Lattimore had never even been a State Department employee, and by July 1950, he was cleared of McCarthy's charges by the Senate Foreign Relations Committee, but not before amassing significant legal fees (he was represented by future Supreme Court Justice Abe Fortas). It was sadly clear to the Lattimores that they would have to sell their half-share in Stefansson's farm, and Stefansson agreed to help by placing an ad in his own name in the *Saturday Review of Literature*.

The only person who answered the ad was Ordway Southard, a former anthropology student at the University of Alaska and a longtime admirer of Stefansson. Southard had done some research in Stefansson's New York library a few years earlier, and had helped move some books and furniture when Stefansson first came to Vermont. He saw the ad and quickly saw an opportunity to have further contact with one of his idols. On June 14, the sale was completed.

Stefansson wrote to Lattimore just after the sale that he had heard through the winter that Southard was a Communist, but "my clippings bureau was then sending me cuttings from the Hearst and Scripps-Howard press saying that I was a Communist....To me this sort of thing was Salem Witchcraft over again, and I perhaps leaned over backward not to be appear to be afflicted with what was increasingly worrying me as mob hysteria." Stefansson astutely went on to warn Lattimore that selling the Stoddard farm to a "Communist" might be used against Lattimore. Lattimore did look into canceling the sale, but his attorney, Abe Fortas, advised him against it, because there was a valid contract.

Evelyn Stefansson did not trust Southard, and wrote in her memoir, "I was angry and hurt that I hadn't prevailed in not wanting to sell to Southard, probably the only time in our long and happy marriage that I blamed 'Stef' and felt he should have listened to me." Evelyn's fears were not just paranoia. What Southard did not tell Stefansson before the sale was that he and his wife Mary had been Communist Party organizers and were still Party members. Further, while in Alabama organizing steel mill workers, Ordway M. Southard had run for governor on the Communist Party ticket in 1942, and Mary Southard ran for state senator as a Communist that same year.

Stefansson described the ensuing confrontation with Southard in his memoir:

> He had not intended to make a secret of his past, he told us. The point simply had not come up. We asked him if he had given a thought, ahead of time, to the possible consequences of his purchase. Well, yes, he had considered the matter, but the fact was, he said, none of us had done anything illegal. On this point, naturally, we had to agree. At the same time, Evelyn and I considered the situation, innocent though it was, most unfortunate for the Lattimores.

Red hunter

The FBI was not alone in watching the Lattimores and Stefanssons. The Southards' past might merely have been the "innocent situation" the Stefanssons imagined, if not for the attention of a local Bethel woman, Lucille Miller, who was known in the area for her extreme anti-communist views. She claimed to have been a former "fellow traveler," but by the mid-1940s dedicated herself to exposing what she saw as left-wing cells that had formed in the Bethel-Randolph area. She wrote frequent letters to prominent conservative syndicated columnists Fulton Lewis Jr. and Westbrook Pegler, and often sent ideas for investigative articles to the Hearst newspaper chain, especially the *Boston Evening Record*.

The influential Pegler quoted Miller in a July 1950 column titled "Vermont Yankees are Suckers for Commies," stating: "The secret of Communist success here has been charm and money. They have bought their way into organizations. They have given farm jobs and contract jobs and washing and ironing work out

Vermont Yankees Are Suckers For Commies

By WESTBROOK PEGLER

NEW YORK — When Alger Hiss was about to go on trial for the second time the defense moved to transfer the case from the Southern District of New York, where the court sits in Manhattan Island, to Vermont which has an old reputation as a Republican state.

Indeed, Vermont and Maine were the only states that voted for Alf Landon, the Republican candidate in the year 1936 when the people had their best real chance to drive the growing pack of traitors out of Washington and re-establish the the republic which was created under the Constitution.

The attempt to take the second Hiss trial up

necticut, including unsuspecting Ridgefield, a town of classical New England beauty, some of the "natives" or work-a-day Yankees who do the odd jobs and the washing and all were easily beguiled by the spurious kindness and generosity of the Communists and fellow-travelers.

"The secret of Communist success here has been charm and money," said the informant mentioned here before. "They have bought their way into organizations. They have given farm jobs and contract jobs and washing and ironing work to the people. They go out of their way to be sympathetic, understanding, to have feeling for the people. I never thought the people of Vermont would fall for it, but they have. They are suckers.

Orlando Sentinel, July 31, 1950

to the people. They go out of their way to be sympathetic and understanding. I never thought the people would fall for it, but they have." The article went on to attack Vermont author Dorothy Canfield Fisher and *Vermont Life* editor Arthur Wallace Peach. "Baloney!" was the title of a *White River Valley Herald* editorial that week. "The Pegler story would be amusing," it stated, "if it were not a skillfully concocted poison." Special targets of Miller's venom were four summer residents of Randolph Center who had been named by disillusioned ex-Communist Whitaker Chambers as members of a spy network that included Alger Hiss (who summered with his family in Peacham, about 5 0 miles to the north). Miller's list of four included Lee Pressman, former lead counsel for the Congress of Industrial Organizations (CIO); Nathan Witt, former secretary general of the National Labor Relations Board; John Abt, Pressman and Witt's attorney (as well as the attorney for the Communist Party); and Abt's sister, Marion Bachrach.

By July 1950, only Pressman still owned property in Vermont, but with Lattimore still on the front pages, *Boston Evening Record* reporter Thomas Riley finally took up Lucille Miller's invitation to see for himself what was happening in Bethel and Randolph Center. He promptly uncovered the Southards' past associations and rushed to press on July 27. Senator McCarthy charged that day on the

Senate floor that Lattimore's property was "in the Hiss area of Vermont" and that the profit Lattimore made on the transaction ($3000 was the figure quoted) was going to the coffers of the Communist Party. Said McCarthy, "There is no secret that the way the Communist Party handles its payoffs and contributions is often by the transfer of property."

When reached in Wellfleet, Massachusetts, Lattimore told the Associated Press, "Since I had to sell my property to meet expenses forced on me by McCarthy's scurrilous attacks, the property was sold to a stranger about whom I knew nothing and of whom I had never heard." The AP reporter then asked Lattimore about a comment by Senator Bourke Hickenlooper of Iowa concerning the possible discovery of uranium oxide on the Vermont farm, increasing its potential value. The reporter noted, "Lattimore laughed loudly and said, 'Just wait till I tell that one to my wife.'"

Soon Stefansson's connection was news as well. A *Rutland Herald* headline of July 29 announced, "Link Explorer With Lattimore Land Deal." Pegler's nationally syndicated column that week focused on the land transaction: "Not only did Lattimore buy an interest in Stefansson's dwelling in a backwoods Vermont spot where Abt, Hiss, Pressman, Witt, and Bachrach had settled, but less than three months later sold it to a buyer described as a prominent Communist."

Once reporters investigated the actual Bethel town records, Senator McCarthy's story of a $3000 profit was easily demolished. Publishers Robert Mitchell of the *Rutland Herald* and John Drysdale of the *White River Valley Herald* and *Bradford Opinion* led the way, with Drysdale summarizing: "No 'excessive profit' indeed no profit at all, was made on the sale of the Stoddard farm. The Lattimores received only half the selling price (Mr. McCarthy take note!)." Mitchell added in a *Rutland Herald* editorial, "One can only conclude that (McCarthy) deliberately withheld the information that Stefansson was the other half-owner of the Bethel farm and that he was to receive half of the sale price, because this would have weakened the accusations and insinuations against Lattimore."

McCarthy Alleges Sale Of Vt. Property By Owen Lattimore To Alleged Reds

The Property, Sold To Married Couple, Is In Bethel—'Hiss Area' McCarthy Says

Burlington Free Press, July 27, 1950

Drysdale led off his editorial in early August with, "The quiet White River towns of Randolph and Bethel have had an introduction in the past week to the slander technique of a certain section of the American press and of Senator McCarthy. Those who will examine the McCarthy accusations…can see a perfect case history of the manner in which individuals can be smeared and slandered in attacks against which they have no defense except the cool common sense of their neighbors." The more conservative *Burlington Free Press* weighed in, "Most hard-headed Vermonters will want to examine with care his present charges before getting into a lather over the situation."

Even the *Burlington Daily News* and *St. Albans Messenger,* owned by William Loeb and perhaps the most conservative papers in Vermont, showed some skepticism. On July 29, both papers ran an exclusive interview with journalist Dorothy Thompson, a syndicated columnist for the Hearst chain and a friend of the Stefanssons who lived in nearby Barnard. Under the headline, "Noted Author Doubts Bethel Is Red Colony," Thompson was quoted as saying she was "extremely skeptical" about McCarthy's charges. "I see nothing strange in the transactions…. I see nothing odd about two old friends buying a farm together and selling it when one of them needs the money."

John Drysdale, publisher of the *White River Valley Herald* and the *Bradford Opinion* (Photo courtesy of *The Herald of Randolph*)

Enter William Gilman

M. Dickey Drysdale, son of John Drysdale and publisher of the *White River Valley Herald* (now the *Herald of Randolph*) since 1975, recalls that his father persuaded Robert Mitchell of the *Rutland Herald* to follow the story further using the advantage of that paper's statewide circulation. Mitchell then took that step, enlisting the collaboration of John S. Hooper of the *Brattleboro Reformer* in commissioning an investigative report by a nationally known journalist, William Gilman. Gilman had worked for *The New York Times* and United

Press International in China and had been a war correspondent for the North American Newspaper Alliance. He was also the author of *Our Hidden Front* (1944), about Alaska's role in World War II, and *The Spy Trap* (1944), a study of pre-war espionage cases.

The series of six articles ran from August 14–19, 1950. Mitchell explained in an editorial of August 12, "There has been so much loose talk and rumor locally, fanned by distorted reports from outside sources, that this newspaper hopes that a constructive service can be performed by presenting a factual report on the communist problem."

The first article was an overview of the situation headlined, "Red Stronghold in State Mostly Hotbed of Gossip and Rumor." Gilman noted, "Although Vermonters know Randolph Center is some 40 miles from Peacham and Bethel is around 50, the Hearst press has ringed all three towns into what it calls Vermont's 'Hiss area.'" He quoted a local farmer, Clifton Chadwick, as saying, "I wouldn't brand anybody a Communist till I knew. It's gotten so that my daughter's ashamed to say she's from Randolph Center." Gilman complimented Drysdale for his editorials "appealing to common sense that have followed the best traditions of a fearless and unbiased press."

The next day's installment was headlined, "US-Born Communists Are Difficult to Spot When They Settle in Vermont," and was a profile of the Southards. "Ordway Southard," said Gilman, "has a

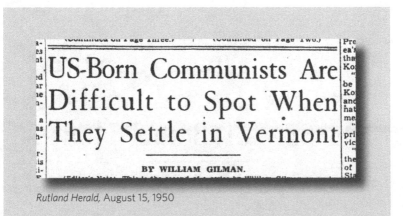

Rutland Herald, August 15, 1950

family background that's as American as corn-on-the-cob.... His equally Red wife, Mary, was Alabama-born, speaks with a cultivated Southern accent, and was graduated from Radcliffe College." The Southards spoke openly to Gilman about their backgrounds, Ordway Southard's anthropological interest in Siberia and in Stefansson's work, and their purchase of the land. But Gilman added, "He spoke willingly at our first meeting....But when he learned that he was being investigated, he changed tactics [and] tried to provoke a brawl with this reporter."

Stefansson was the subject of the next article, "Famous Arctic Explorer Sets the Record Straight on Sale of Bethel House," with a full history of the various transactions over the years. On day four, the series featured a profile of Lucille Miller under the headline, "Reformed 'Fellow Traveler' Finds More Reds in Bethel Than the FBI Does in State." In this article, Miller traced the Randolph Center "red cell" activity back to a free-thinking farmer, Closson Gilbert, who had gone away to Chicago to study for the ministry, had come under the influence of social reformer Jane Addams, and had returned to Vermont to promote leftist ideas. She was quoted as saying, "You have to go to Randolph Center and take your butterfly net....The place is crawling with Reds."

"Randolph Center Residents Reply to Communist Charge" was the headline of the fifth article, in which Gilman interviewed targets

Famous Arctic Explorer Sets the Record Straight On Sale of Bethel House

BY WILLIAM GILMAN.

Rutland Herald, August 16, 1950

Tony Hiss: A Refuge in "Hiss Country"

Tony Hiss was seven years old when his father, Alger Hiss, was involved in one of the most controversial episodes of the Cold War. Hiss was accused of being a spy for the Soviet Union and was convicted, after three separate trials, not for espionage but for perjury. He was sent to Lewisburg Federal Penitentiary in Pennsylvania. In his memoir of those years, The View from Alger's Window, *Tony Hiss remembers with fondness his time in Peacham, Vermont. The family had been summering in Peacham for many years and had developed strong friendships. The "Great Span" that Tony mentions in this excerpt comes from a phrase of his father's, and refers to the passing of knowledge through generations.*

At the time [of Alger Hiss' trials] I had, for my own good it had been thought, been taken out of the picture. Prossy [Priscilla Hiss, Alger's wife] and Alger didn't see why my life should be disrupted just because they were in trouble. It was explained to me that this would be more fun—and in some ways it was. The first trial, which everyone assumed would be the only trial, started, conveniently, just as second grade was ending. So I was sent up to Peacham for the next six weeks, which is where I loved to be and would have expected to be anyway; my mother later remembered that on the way to the train station, I proudly told the cabdriver, "I am going to the place I dream about in the winter." In Peacham, I was under the care of Rena Hunter—"Aunt Rena" to me—the elderly Peacham woman I loved more dearly than anyone in the world, because her bony hugs were the most sheltering thing in the world. She'd lived with us the past several summers first as a housekeeper, then as a friend, and finally as a member of the family; she was in fact old enough to be one of Alger's or Prossy's aunts.

Thanks to Aunt Rena and several of her Peacham near contemporaries, including Elsie Choate, owner of the Choate Inn (where Alger and Prossy had stayed during the 1930s), and Ernest Brown, sexton of the Congregational Church, I felt welcomed inside a sturdy, ongoing, northern Vermont form of the Great Span. I already sensed that the old Vermonters who befriended me were no longer walking in step with many postwar Americans who, although my elders, were the Peacham people's juniors.

of Lucille Miller. Most, like farmers Harry Cooley and Morris LaFrance, had landed on her list due to their public support of the left-leaning Henry Wallace in the presidential race of 1948. Gilman also noted that the town's State School of Agriculture (now Vermont Technical College) was undergoing its own controversy, as college president George Webster was described as attempting to force the resignation of faculty member Philip Hodgdon, after Hodgdon had publicly asked Lucille Miller for proof of her charges.

The final article, "Vermonters Frown on Use of Violence to Rid State of Communists They Hate," took a sampling of local opinion. "A vote would show close to 100 percent of local folks opposed to having real Communists around. But that also brings up the stubborn problem of protecting the man called 'Communist' when he isn't one." The seven closing paragraphs are given over to J. Edgar Hoover's instructions—verbatim—on how to report suspicions to the FBI, an irony foreshadowing the Bureau's methods of hounding non-communists such as Stefansson and Lattimore, with the latter's file alone growing to 38,000 pages.

In the following two weeks, there were several letters to the *Reformer* and the *Herald,* most supportive of the investigative series. One person who signed anonymously as "Freedom Loving," said, "In the last few weeks, we in Vermont have been unfortunate enough to see firsthand how our freedom can be lost without a single Russian soldier standing over us." Another letter, from W. W. Ballard of Norwich, began: "Thank you for having sponsored the Gilman articles about the Red menace in the heart of Vermont.... Your account of a state of mind in the affected communities deserves a good deal of thought because the same thing could happen anywhere in these nervous times."

By the end of August, the controversy over the land sale had disappeared from local front pages and editorial columns. Evelyn Stefansson wrote to Eleanor Lattimore in early September that "everywhere we hear words of praise for Owen's wonderful fight [against McCarthy's charges]."

Ordway and Mary Southard stayed on at the Stoddard farm, though the Stefanssons refused to speak to them after that sum-

Boston Daily Herald, July 28, 1950

mer's events. The Southards maintained a low profile until an incident in April 1952 put them back in the news; their pickup truck was vandalized with a hatchet in broad daylight. A local man, Thomas Petrocelli, was charged with public intoxication, breach of peace, and malicious destruction of property, and another Bethel resident, Wilfred Loura, was alleged to have struck Ray Brink, a Southard neighbor who was attempting to escort Mrs. Southard away from the scene.

In a letter to the *Rutland Herald* several days later, Lucille Miller asked to be charged as well by State's Attorney Lewis Springer: "I take complete responsibility for this incident and all others like it because if it were not for my 1950 attack on this Communist colony, nobody would have known that the Southards were Communists."

This letter was on Stefansson's mind when the Lattimores proposed a visit that July, shortly after Dwight Eisenhower's selection of Richard Nixon for his running mate. "Much as I want to see you," Stefansson wrote, "I feel you must do your own judging on whether Mrs. Miller is likely to send in 'information' and how likely the Nixon wing of the Republicans is to pick up and use her imaginings in a further attack on you.... If you decide that coming here is no more dangerous than not coming, we can get up some presentable wakes here for the demise of American liberty." There is no evidence of what the Lattimores decided.

Stefansson's fears were well founded, for by 1952, Lattimore's troubles had increased. Although he had been cleared by the Senate Judiciary Committee in July 1950, Lattimore's defiant stance towards Senator McCarthy created new enemies. Senator Pat McCarran of Nevada, chairman of the Senate Internal Security Subcommittee, took up McCarthy's charges against him and, with help from the FBI, added fresh ones. Lattimore was forced to spend the next five years on leave from Johns Hopkins, fighting charges that he had lied to Congress. The charges were eventually dismissed in 1955. He went on to reclaim his reputation as a renowned scholar, as head of the Asian Studies Department at Leeds University, England, and was an early opponent of the Vietnam War. He lived to see Richard Nixon go to China, and revisited China and Mongolia before his death in 1988.

Although the Southards kept their property until 1964, they left Bethel shortly after the vandalism incident and continued their travels. During their stay in Hawaii, they became deeply involved in Asian culture and philosophy; "Ordway" and "Mary" became "O" and "Malia." It was as "O Mabson Southard" that Southard became well known in the poetry world as both a haiku poet and an expert on the form.

Lucille Miller and her husband Manuel, emboldened by letters of support she received from all over the country, started publishing a mimeographed broadside in 1952 called *Green Mountain Rifleman*. Their targets were communists, Jews, and Vermonters such as Education Commissioner A. John Holden (although not Jewish himself, Holden was accused of "following the B'nai Brith [sic] line"). The Millers made headlines again in 1955 when Federal marshals stormed their house and arrested both for urging young men to defy the authority of the federal government by refusing to register for the draft.

Shortly after his proposed Encyclopedia Arctica was scuttled by the Department of Navy in 1949, Vilhjalmur Stefansson donated his entire collection of Arctic literature (running to over 20,000 volumes) to Dartmouth College. In 1951, he was offered a position there as founding director of the Northern and Polar Studies Program, now known as the Institute of Arctic Studies. Although he and Evelyn kept their Bethel property until his death in 1962, the "Southard Affair" left lingering bitterness, and the Stefanssons spent most of their time in Hanover. But they weren't yet through with being subjects of suspicion. In 1954, New Hampshire's headline-hunting Attorney General Louis Wyman, accused them both, with little success, of being communist sympathizers. Stefansson's memoir, published posthumously in 1974, had a chapter on the Lattimore episode that concluded with these words: "Even today, the nightmare [of those years] reappears, reminding us that the McCarthy type of persecution is a sinister poison that affects the innocent perhaps more than the guilty."

Professor Alex Novikoff, who was fired from the University of
Vermont for his political associations (courtesy of University of
Vermont Special Collections)

CHAPTER FOUR / 1953

DEFENDING
ALEX NOVIKOFF:
THE LEGACY OF
ARNOLD SCHEIN

"It was a shabby performance all around. ...The trustees and the administration disgraced themselves and the University." The speaker was Arnold Schein on June 11, 1988, as he looked back thirty-five years to one of Vermont's major Red Scare controversies involving Alex Novikoff, a biochemistry professor at the University of Vermont's Medical School. Novikoff had taken the Fifth Amendment during a Senate hearing into Communist Party influence at Brooklyn College, where he had taught before coming to Vermont. He was subsequently fired by the trustees of the University of Vermont. Arnold Schein never lost his anger at the injustice visited on his friend and colleague and welcomed the chance to address the "Vermont in the McCarthy Era" conference in 1988 and to tell the story to a new generation.

Alex Novikoff, the man at the center of this storm, was six years old when his parents emigrated from Ukraine in 1919. He attended Columbia University and hoped to become a doctor but came up against the restrictive quota on Jewish admissions to the medical school. He then became a graduate student in biology at Columbia, and it was during this period, in 1935, that he joined the Communist Party. While teaching biology at Brooklyn College a few years later, he joined a group of younger instructors fighting for better faculty working conditions, merit-based promotion, and greater job security.

"I first met Alex in New York City when we were both officers of the American Association of Scientific Workers, a so-called popular front group," recalled Schein in 1988. "During World War II, the Russians were our allies, and it was not unusual for left liberals like myself and Communist Party members like Novikoff to work together."

In Schein's retelling, he recognized Novikoff as someone from a similar background; both were New York City Jews of immigrant parents. "I was truly a peer having grown up in the same environment as Alex," said Schein. "We were both brought up with social compassion, and never forgot the poor and deprived. My fellow students of every political party or fashion had one thing in common: they had great sympathy for the underprivileged, the blacks, for all minorities and working people."

After Schein joined the faculty of the University of Vermont, he persuaded Novikoff to leave New York City and come to Vermont in 1947. At the University of Vermont, Novikoff's main affiliation was with the Department of Pathology, but he also had a connection with the Department of Biochemistry, which is where he and Schein collaborated on a scientific paper.

A political past catches up

Novikoff did not lead an active political life in Burlington, Schein recalled. Like many of his peers, he had become disillusioned with the Soviet model and with Stalin's rule. He was devoted to his work and to his family; at the time, his young son Kenny was seriously ill with kidney disease. But his political past caught up with him in April 1953, when the Senate Internal Security Committee, headed by William Jenner of Indiana, began an investigation into Commu-

Arnold Schein, a colleague of Novikoff's and his primary
defender on the UVM faculty (courtesy of Susan Schein)

nist Party influence at Brooklyn College. Jenner was just as viru-
lently anti-communist as McCarthy, but was looked upon by many
Republicans as less of a loose cannon.

Novikoff's name was already known to the Jenner Committee
from previous hearings in New York City in the early 1940s. The
Rapp-Coudert Committee, an investigating committee of the New
York State Legislature, subpoenaed and interrogated more than 500
faculty, staff, and students from New York City's four public universities probing for political affiliation with the Communist Party or
non-cooperation with the legislative inquiry. Novikoff, along with
more than 40 other Brooklyn College colleagues, narrowly escaped
dismissal due to the Board of Higher Education's "two-witness"

UVM Professor Balks At Jenner Red Quiz

Burlington Free Press, April 4, 1953

rule in cases of suspected perjury; only one witness testified against him. When Novikoff was again named as a Communist Party member by a former Brooklyn College colleague before the Jenner Committee thirteen years later, it marked the beginning of the end of his tenured professorship at the University of Vermont.

Novikoff had decided to tell the senators what they wanted to know about his past, but when they requested he name other members of the Communist Party at Brooklyn College, Novikoff refused, citing the Fifth Amendment. Schein immediately sensed what Novikoff faced during and after the Jenner hearings. "McCarthyism stirred into flame the glowing embers of fear of communism that pervaded our country in the early 1950s," he said at the 1988 conference. "It was thought that young and susceptible minds could easily be manipulated by devilishly unscrupulous professors of such subjects of biology and chemistry."

During this era it was not enough to admit one's past Communist Party membership. "Alex had failed the litmus test of identifying Communists as proof of severing his ties with the Communist Party," wrote Schein in 1987, on the occasion of Novikoff's death. "It was made clear to him that he could escape his certain fate by acceding to the Jenner Committee's demand to name names. His moral code would not permit him to do that." Schein also knew Novikoff's legal reason for taking the Fifth: a witness could be cited for perjury if any of the committee's stable of paid informers and ex-communists contradicted his testimony. There was an additional dilemma that many witnesses—whether in academia, Hollywood, or elsewhere— faced: courts had ruled that a First Amendment plea would not protect anyone from a Contempt of Congress citation (William Hinton, as we will see in Chapter Five, was in a similar bind). As Novikoff later explained at his UVM hearing: "Under the present circumstances, it is virtually impossible to make the (Jenner) committee believe that there is a difference between a communist who would not stop at anything to overthrow our government and the communists who out of confusion, out of sincerity, have seen only certain aspects of communist activity.... You cannot hope to draw that distinction before the committee. So when you say, name names, any name, your name is immediately put into the category of those who would not stop at anything."

Once Novikoff came back to Burlington after testifying, the question became whether the University of Vermont would take any action. As Ellen Schrecker points out in *No Ivory Tower,* her study of McCarthyism in academia, universities were under no obligation to act after an individual professor testified before a committee. In response to the fear of the times, however, most universities decided to set up procedures for firing faculty members who did not comply with investigators. "Without the almost automatic imposition of sanctions on the people who had been identified as politically undesirable, the whole anti-communist structure would have crumbled," writes Schrecker. "Records of proceedings show how the academy, an institution ostensibly dedicated to intellectual freedom, collaborated in curtailing that freedom."

Spiraling downward at UVM

Schrecker describes a chronology of what unfolded at the University of Vermont. The Federal Bureau of Investigation notified Vermont governor Lee Emerson, who pressured University president Carl Borgmann to convene a committee to pass judgment on Novikoff. That committee, chaired by Father Robert Joyce (later Bishop of the Diocese of Burlington), voted 5-1 to retain Novikoff. Emerson then persuaded the trustees to form their own committee, with the express purpose of overriding the Joyce committee's recommendation. According to David Holmes, author of a comprehensive study of the Novikoff case, *Stalking the Academic Communist,* Governor Emerson threatened to cut off University funds if Novikoff were not dismissed. Emerson told President Borgmann that the public needed to be reassured that the "faculty is 100 percent pro-American and anti-communist." Holmes added, "Not many universities could have withstood that pressure."

As Schein put it, "I witnessed the travail and agony of the president (Borgmann) as the administration gradually became the accomplices of the Jenner Committee." Schein found it hard to believe that the University of Vermont was debating whether

Clergy Urge UVM To Retain Novikoff

Burlington Free Press, July 9, 1953

to dismiss a stellar member of the faculty and an outstanding researcher for political positions he had taken years earlier. "So it all boiled down to you could be an excellent teacher, an innovator, perform all your university duties and responsibilities in an exemplary fashion and this would count for nothing. If you avail yourself of your constitutional rights, you would be fired from UVM."

Schein was bitterly disappointed when his own university gave in to pressures faced by other academic institutions. "Universities found themselves unwittingly on the firing line with powerful social forces, alumni, the media, state legislatures and governors demanding action and calling for identification of and punitive action against known Communists," he later wrote. "While I protested the wrongs visited upon my colleague at UVM, I was also concerned with the larger issue—the willing collaboration of the university with the forces of reaction, using unconstitutional tools of repression, which undermined the very nature of the university."

Additional pressure on the University was applied through strident editorials by the *Burlington Daily News,* and less strident but equally negative ones in the more influential *Burlington Free Press.* When a group of 26 Burlington-area religious figures signed a letter in support of Novikoff, the *Daily News* editorialized, "'In times such as these, when the nation faces destruction by the sympathetic and very able plotting of Communist agents and spies, such judgment on the part of the clergy is very miserable indeed." In another of his trademark front-page editorials, *Daily News* publisher William Loeb stated, "Congress and the public have a right to know, whether Novikoff is attempting to influence the minds of countless numbers of individuals in favor of the Communist conspiracy to destroy this nation."

The only editor statewide to express support for Novikoff was Bernard O'Shea, the publisher/editor of the weekly *Swanton Courier.* The reaction to O'Shea's support brought the suggestion that the *Courier* was "communist-minded" and that the editor was flawed by his education and by his out-of-state origins. One letter writer said, "It is known that O'Shea has a college education and it is more than likely that he received some instruction about Communism. He brings those thoughts here to Vermont." (See Chapter Seven for more on Bernard O'Shea.)

The "Russian-born" Novikoff

Another factor in the Novikoff case, though no one would discuss it publicly at the time, is what Susan Schein, Arnold Schein's daughter, called the "low-grade and pervasive anti-Semitism" that she and her family experienced in Burlington. Novikoff, whose name often appeared in the news with the descriptor "Russian-born," a barely disguised code for "alien and untrustworthy," and his vocal supporters, Schein and Rabbi Max Wall, stood out in Yankee New England. As David Holmes wrote, "It appears that many Vermonters of the early 1950s may have carried inarticulated suspicions about a man who was thought to be 'Russian,' Jewish, and a suspected Communist."

Max Wall: Another Novikoff Ally

Max Wall was the rabbi at Burlington's Ohavi Zedek Synagogue from 1946 to 1987. According to his 2009 obituary in the Burlington Free Press, "He was a beloved religious leader, teacher and a man whose counsel helped many people in his congregation and the larger community. First and foremost he wanted to be remembered as a man who loved people, a humanist, and in kind, this love was returned multifold." He was one of Alex Novikoff's chief defenders in the Burlington community. He spoke to Mark Greenberg for the Vermont Historical Society's Green Mountain Chronicles *radio program in 1988.*

I knew Alex Novikoff because I was involved with the hospital and the University; I used to occasionally lecture to students at the Medical School as well. So I got to know a lot of the Jewish faculty on campus. I had no close relationship with Alex because he wasn't a very institutionally religiously-oriented individual. But then I heard that he had refused to answer questions to the Jenner Committee. Shortly after that I was called by the late Bishop Vedder Van Dyke who was the Episcopal Bishop for the state of Vermont and who was very much upset with this prosecution. And he got together with me and with Bishop Robert Joyce. I was sort of made an unofficial Bishop of the Jewish community and the three of us were in agreement that this was an outrage. We got, I think, most of the clergy in the area to support us.

Hundreds of thousands of Americans might have been in Novikoff's place simply because in the 1930s, people were looking to solutions to problems that no one seemed to have, and if there was a promise that seemed to be a false promise, so many us said, 'wait a minute, this is the wrong door, I made a mistake.' Alex was a man who was a fundamentally dedicated scientist, no other concern whatever.

Schein and fellow Novikoff supporters on the faculty such as William Van Robertson tried to rally their colleagues, but to no avail. Schein recalled, "Other faculty kept their distance, though I detected a groundswell of resentment that the University was giving in so easily." With the help of several allies in the community and on the faculty, he distributed the text of Novikoff's testimony before the trustees' final vote, in which Novikoff had denied doing anything political since moving to Vermont. The close of the academic year also complicated matters. The term had ended, with faculty and students dispersed by the time the committee's report came out in mid-June. No minutes of the trustees' meeting had been made public. "The faculty as a whole could do little more than express concern," said Schein, who was himself a member of UVM's Faculty Senate. He sent letter after letter to the American Association of University Professors (AAUP) and even volunteered to be their field representative for the case. But apart from a brief AAUP visit to Vermont, no support materialized, and with Father Joyce casting the lone dissenting vote, Novikoff was officially fired on September 5.

Not surprisingly, Schein himself came under suspicion, learning later that the FBI kept tabs on him. Since he was never a member of the Communist Party, he was not named by any informants, and was never called to testify at any venue. According to his daughter Susan, he believed that his outspokenness cost him the loss of several friendships and advancement at the University (he later went on to teach at San Jose State in California). "In a psychological sense, he felt he had lost his home at the University."

"For them," she said, "the case inscribed a bright line between those of their friends and colleagues who had the moral courage to stand up and speak out in the face of opprobrium and possible consequence and those who did not." Long after the event itself, "My mom and dad still parsed their acquaintances: who took a stand? Who fell back, hoping for invisibility and safety, deep and silent in the background?" Those who, like her parents, had worked hard for justice, such as Rabbi Wall in particular, earned their undying admiration.

"My father was fierce and fearless in those moments, charged up for academic freedom," recalls Susan. "I think my father always felt that during the Novikoff case, he became the best person he could be."

Unlike many victims of the Red Scare, Novikoff went on to significant professional success, becoming a researcher at the newly founded Albert Einstein College of Medicine in New York City. Knowing of Einstein's concern about the national anti-Communist campaign, Novikoff had written to Einstein shortly before his dismissal. "Because I exercised my constitutional right in refusing to answer certain questions, I am being dismissed," Novikoff wrote. "Would any position be open to me at the new medical school bearing your great name?" While at Einstein, he achieved renown in the scientific community for his research on a biochemical approach to the study of enzymes. In 1958, he was promoted to full professor and was awarded a major research grant from the National Institutes of Health.

He returned to Burlington in 1983 to receive an honorary UVM degree and received an official apology from the university. Showing a surprising generosity of spirit, Novikoff willed his scientific papers to UVM. Two years after his death in 1987, on the occasion of UVM receiving those papers, the *Burlington Free Press* ran an editorial formally apologizing for their role. "The University of Vermont was wrong in 1953," the editorial stated. "So was the *Burlington Free Press* editorial page, which saw Communists in every closet, and failed to defend Novikoff's rights and endorsed his firing. The arrival of Alex Novikoff's papers renews our regret that we are 36 years late."

At the 1988 conference, Schein concluded his remarks by paying tribute to his friend and colleague: "He had a great sense of ethics, and was twice the man any of the people who sat in judgment were. All he wanted was a chance to continue his work in society and to continue to do his job." That job might have brought significant prestige to the University of Vermont, had they not succumbed to the fears of the times.

Forgiving Gesture Brings Novikoff Papers to UVM

Rutland Herald, January 31, 1989

Wiliam Hinton's classic study *Fanshen*, published by Monthly Review Press.

CHAPTER FIVE / 1953–1954

FROM "PEIPING" TO PUTNEY: THE HINTON FAMILY AND THE RED SCARE

During the month of September 1949, headlines in the *Brattleboro Reformer* mirrored others the world over: "Communists Take Over Peiping"; "Mao Tze-tung China's New Ruler." This epochal event opened another front in the nascent Cold War and further stoked American fears of communism's spreading threat. It also created ripples that were felt in Brattleboro's northerly neighbor, Putney.

Putney, then and now a town of approximately 2,500 residents, has had a surprisingly wide connection with world affairs, especially during the tumultuous early years of the Cold War. This was due to the influence of the Putney School and the children of its founder, Carmelita Hinton. When two of her children, William and Joan, became fervent supporters of the new Chinese government, the resulting headlines catapulted both the small town and the even smaller school into the national spotlight. For the first time since the Owen Lattimore controversy of 1950 (see Chapter Three), Vermont was again in the glare of national media.

To understand the outsize impact of the Putney School, one must go back to its remarkable founder. During Carmelita Chase Hinton's second year at Bryn Mawr College in 1912, she read an essay by the philosopher William James that changed her life. As she remembered the words years later, "If you find yourself deeply stirred by what you read and see, it is harmful to you to let this emotion dissipate itself without resultant action. Do something." The "something" that she did years later was founding the Putney School, a pioneering experiment in progressive education whose impact has stretched far beyond its borders.

Hinton, an Omaha native, had a further social and educational awakening as an undergraduate when she realized that the only African-Americans she encountered were those serving meals and cleaning rooms. "I don't think there was one black girl attending the college," she said. "They were there to serve us, the elite. We were parasites on them." As a result of this jarring realization, self-reliance became a vital part of her philosophy. The philosophies of William James, John Dewey, and other progressive educators who believed that children should learn by doing and through real-life experiences instead of by rote learning only reinforced that principle.

After college, she worked in Chicago at Jane Addams' Hull House, one of the pioneering "settlement houses" that provided various community services to poverty-stricken urban areas in the United States. She married patent lawyer Sebastian Hinton in 1916. After her husband's untimely death in 1923, she spent time both traveling with her three young children, Jean, William, and Joan and teaching second grade for several years at Shady Hill School in Cambridge, Massachusetts. The idea for a school based on Dewey's ideas came to her in 1934. She bought a dairy farm in Putney and, with fifty-four students and a small faculty, began her coeducational school in converted farm buildings.

"I had this idea that the world was a pretty unpleasant place," she said years later. "I thought education could help make children less greedy, less self-centered. Many of the young people who came to the school might become government leaders when they were of age. And they might have a different, more ethical slant on our problems as a result of this education."

Putney's program stressed, along with conventional academics and athletics, an unconventional self-reliance in learning. Unorthodox, too, was the required farm work and manual labor. Until her retirement in 1955, "Mrs. H.," as she was known, was in the forefront of educators who embraced independent study, team teaching, community involvement, and an evaluation system without grades. As the reputation of the school grew, it enrolled the children of nationally known figures such as architect Norman Bel Geddes, educator James Conant, and attorney Helen Lehman Buttenweiser. The school's philosophy was an inspiration not only for generations of students, but also for Carmelita Hinton's own three children.

The Hinton children: Jean, William, and Joan

Jean Hinton, the eldest of Carmelita's children, was too old to be in Putney's first class, but nevertheless absorbed the lessons of self-reliance and social commitment. She attended Bennington College, another southern Vermont institution influenced by John Dewey's educational principles. After graduating in 1938, she lived with migrant farmers, collecting data for the Farm Security Administration under the directorship of Nathan Silvermaster, later accused of being a communist sympathizer. Like her mother, she was roused to activism by the unequal treatment of African-Americans. She once said that her mission in life became clear to her one day in 1941 when she convinced a group of white activists to eat at a blacks-only government cafeteria in Washington, D.C. "The memory of that experience still stirs my adrenaline," she said in 1997. "I was indignant at the injustices in the world."

In the early 1940s she became president of the Washington, D.C., union local of the Federal Workers of America, and she helped organize western Pennsylvania in 1948 for Henry Wallace's Progressive Party presidential campaign. Her file kept by the FBI runs to 250 pages. It covers not only her own political activities but also her personal connections from her job in the Farm Security Administration working under Silvermaster. In 1948, the so-called Red Spy Queen, Elizabeth Bentley, had named Silvermaster as the leader of a group of U.S. government workers who were sympathetic to the Soviet Union, though he was never charged with spying. Anyone who worked with Silvermaster, especially those like Jean Hinton who knew him socially as well, came under particular scrutiny.

The union activities of Jean's husband Steven Rosner, an organizer with the Pittsburgh branch of the Electrical Workers of America, were also noted by the FBI. In 1953, the FBI recommended putting Jean Hinton Rosner on the Security Index, a list of 12,000 Americans to be put in "permanent detention" should the need arise. Jean's daughter Marni Rosner still remembers being taught as a young child how to recognize FBI men at the front door ("creased pants and shiny shoes") and how to send them away ("my mother's out shopping").

William, Carmelita Hinton's middle child, graduated from the Putney School in 1936 as part of its first class. Accepted at Harvard College, he postponed matriculation and instead traveled in the Far East for a year, supporting himself with odd jobs and developing his lifelong interest in China. He attended Harvard from 1937 to 1939, then transferred to Cornell for its agricultural programs, graduating in 1941 with a degree in agronomy and dairy husbandry.

After being inspired by Edgar Snow's 1937 book *Red Star Over China,* William Hinton returned to China during World War II as a propaganda analyst for the Office of War Information and again in 1947 as a tractor technician for the United Nations Relief and Rehabilitation Administration (UNRRA). When the United Nations program ended, he stayed on as an English teacher and agricultural adviser in rural Long Bow Village, later to become well-known as the setting for his book, *Fanshen.* In the years of upheaval following World War II, William observed both the corruption of Chiang Kai-Shek's Nationalist forces and the end of a feudal society in communist-controlled areas. He became a passionate supporter of Mao Zedong's revolution, later noting that "the power of the revolution to inspire and remold stirred me." William Hinton was one of the few Americans to see the changes wrought on a local level by the

Carmelita Hinton at the Putney School, 1949
(photo by Rudolph Furrer, courtesy of Marni Rosner)

communist takeover, and he took more than a thousand pages of notes on the massive land reform transformation that he witnessed.

William's younger sister, Joan, who graduated from the Putney School in 1939, also saw firsthand the Chinese transformation of 1949. Like her sister Jean, she went to Bennington College, but later transferred to Cornell. Cornell, however, would not accept a woman for postgraduate study in physics so she enrolled at the University of Wisconsin. Following graduation she was recruited, at age twenty-two, to join the team of physicists at Los Alamos, New Mexico, who were working on atomic weapons. She was there when the Trinity atomic bomb test was carried out on July 16, 1945. "We first felt the heat on our faces, then we saw what looked like a sea of light," she told the *South China Morning Post* in 2008. "It was gradually sucked into an awful purple glow that went up and up into a mushroom cloud. It looked beautiful as it lit up the morning sun."

Joan Hinton, like several other scientists working at Los Alamos, thought that the bomb would be used only for a demonstration explosion to force a Japanese surrender. She was horrified when it was actually used on Hiroshima and Nagasaki in August 1945. Though she did briefly go to the University of Chicago for more graduate work with Enrico Fermi in 1946, she then abandoned the field of nuclear physics and became an outspoken peace activist. As a member of the recently formed Federation of American Scientists, she took part in a campaign to send the mayors of every major city in the United States a small glass case filled with glassified desert sand and a note asking whether they wanted their cities to suffer the same fate. After unsuccessfully lobbying the government for the internationalization of nuclear power, she found another outlet for her political interests.

Her brother William's roommate at Cornell, Erwin ("Sid") Engst, had grown up on a New York dairy farm and, like William, had been working with the UNRRA in China since 1946. A budding romance between Sid and Joan, together with William's own enthusiasm about China, led Joan to become involved with Chinese child welfare activities organized by Soong Ching-ling, the respected widow of President Sun Yat-sen. Joan traveled to Shanghai in 1948 to work directly with Madame Soong, who was also a key figure in establishing contacts with the insurgent Chinese communists. In 1949, Joan moved to Yan'an, Mao Zedong's rural headquarters, to marry Sid.

A potential traitor

As postwar relations with the Soviet Union deteriorated, Joan Hinton's decision to leave the atomic program and go to China eventually sounded alerts at the FBI. The communist takeover of 1949 had sent shock waves through the American government, with conservatives demanding to know "who lost China." Any official (such as Owen Lattimore, John Stewart Service, and John Carter Vincent) who had gone on record in favor of negotiating with the communists came under suspicion.

Although Joan Hinton and her new husband were farming in the Chinese countryside without access to electricity or radios, she was viewed in official U.S. government circles as a potential traitor, especially after she was spotted giving a toast at a 1952 peace conference in Beijing. The FBI began to monitor Jean Hinton Rosner's mail in order to keep track of Joan; they also began to take a closer look at the activities of their brother. When William Hinton returned to Vermont from China in August 1953, the FBI was waiting. He recalled the scene years later:

> My mother and sister Jean met me at the dock and they had in their hand a magazine called *Real Magazine* and it had an article about my younger sister Joan entitled, 'The Atom Spy That Got Away,' written by the head of Naval Intelligence in the Pacific Theater in the Second World War. This article said that my sister Joan, who worked with Fermi at Los Alamos in making the atom bomb, escaped to China and gave them all the atomic secrets and I was the guy who arranged all this. My mother and sister were a little pale and asked, 'What did you come home for?' I said, 'Well, I'm not worried about anything.' And I figured if they were serious, if the ruling class wanted to do me in, it wouldn't be in *Real Magazine*.

But William Hinton had come back to the United States at a particularly fearful moment. Just two months earlier, Julius and Ethel Rosenberg had been executed after being convicted for passing atomic secrets, and William had underestimated the level of FBI interest. He arrived in Newport, Vermont, to discover that the U.S. Customs Agency had seized 112 books and pamphlets printed in Chinese and "nine pounds of single-spaced, typewritten, carbon copy on very thin paper including reports of activities in China." William had intended these notes to be the basis of a planned book about how the Chinese revolution came to Long Bow Village in Shanxi Province.

In William Hinton's retelling, he asked the customs officer if he made a habit of breaking into people's things and taking whatever he wanted: "He said, 'Oh, we never break into anything, we have keys that fit everything.' That was the beginning of the harassment I experienced." For the next year, William used Putney as his home base, where he was convinced that his mail was being opened and

William Hinton (left) and his attorney, Milton Friedman, in Washington D.C., 1954 (Associated Press photo)

his phone tapped (a suspicion later borne out in more than 20,000 pages of FBI files). He recalled a close Putney friend saying, "You're welcome to visit, but come after dark." Undeterred, he embarked on a barnstorming tour of the country (300 lectures by his count), speaking to any group curious to learn about events in China since 1949.

The FBI soon determined that "no evidence in subject's luggage indicates that he is recruited by the Chinese Communist government for subversive activities in the US or to act as an agent or propagandist for the Chinese Communist government." But despite this conclusion, the notes were not returned. Instead, they were sent to the Senate's Committee on Internal Security, chaired by Senator James Eastland of Mississippi. Soon after, William Hinton was subpoenaed to appear for a televised hearing in July 1954, ostensibly as part of a Senate investigation of those working with government agencies (in his case, the UNRRA) who had appeared to support "Red China."

The hearing came at a difficult time for the Putney School. Although the children of such establishment figures as diplomat Ellsworth Bunker and CIA chief Allen Dulles had attended, Putney School could not seem to escape its reputation as a place with leftist leanings. Carmelita Hinton had become inured over the years to the attacks and insinuations that her school was a radical hotbed, nor did she attempt to deflect those charges. The school (known as "Red Hill" by some locals) had provided a haven first for those fleeing fascism and then for those fired by other institutions for left-wing associations. Just two months before William's testimony, Carmelita had weathered a storm of suspicion when three Quaker teachers at the school refused to take a Vermont Board of Education loyalty oath. The issue subsided when the state adjusted the require-ment to a simple "affirmation" rather than a sworn oath.[1]

By that summer, Senator Joseph McCarthy himself had been discredited. The disastrous Army-McCarthy hearings had run from April through June and McCarthy had come under attack from a growing number of senators, chief among them Vermont senator Ralph Flanders. But the widespread anti-communist crusade itself was still in full swing, with Eastland one of its leaders in Washing-ton, along with Senators Pat McCarran of Nevada, Edward Jenner of Indiana, and Herman Welker of Idaho.

"An idealist gone wrong"

The headline in the *Brattleboro Reformer* summed up the testy proceedings at the hearing: "Hinton Balky at Red Probe." William later concluded that much of the hostility of the hearing was due to the inability of Senator Eastland and others to accept the new China. "The Americans were thrown out in 1949…it had to be a

----

[1]One person keeping an eye on the activities in Putney was a New Hampshire neigh-bor, Herbert Philbrick, a former advertising man turned FBI undercover agent whose exploits were the basis of the hit television series *I Led Three Lives*. Recently a Putney School graduate doing research at the Library of Congress discovered a Herbert Philbrick file with several pages of handwritten notes on the school's progressive bent and shared her find with Putney's current head, Emily Jones. Some of the notes read: "There are 20,000 volumes in the library and not a pro-American book in the entire lot." "No ethics… . No religion…Sunday evenings there is always a talk." "Owen Lattimore [Far East expert under attack by Senator McCarthy] graduation speaker."

conspiracy," he said. And if it was a conspiracy, then William Hinton himself was a living example of treason. He also concluded at the time that the committee was using him to get publicity for its anti-communist crusade, and he came to Washington ready to fight back. He was also reluctant to get anyone else—such as his sister Joan—in trouble. A week after his testimony, he explained his motives in a letter that was sent to the Putney School community:

> What the Senators were interested in was to attack me for having lived and worked in China, and for having spoken favorably of it since I returned home. My hearing showed that sympathy for the Chinese peasants and advocacy for peaceful relations is suspicious. Faced with this inquisition into matters which are of no proper concern to the Senate, I could not, in good conscience, go along with it. I could not bring myself to answer questions about American persons, associations, and organizations—especially those which sponsored me—which might conceivably become targets of unprincipled attacks.

William Hinton said in this letter that he would have preferred to use the First Amendment, but investigating committees of Congress did not recognize a refusal to answer on that ground; he might well have been jailed for contempt. Though he was prepared to go to jail, he argued, "I did not want the senators to silence me so casually." On the advice of his attorney, Milton Friedman (not the noted economist of the same name), he instead invoked the Fifth Amendment, with its right to prevent self-incrimination: "I felt that to abandon a constitutional right which is among the most precious we have simply because certain senators have made some headway towards bringing it into disrepute, would be an unjustified surrender to hysteria."

William concluded his letter: "In thinking over the events of that day, my chief regret is that I did not sufficiently challenge the committee members on their whole un-American procedure, on their right to ask such questions as they ask. On their right to harass innocent people as they do."

Although he was ultimately able to give a thorough account of his agricultural work in China (which Eastland termed "the autobiography of a traitor" in *U.S. News & World Report*), he refused to answer seventy-nine questions, including whether he had been a member of the Communist Party. He declined as well to answer questions about his sister Joan. This excerpt from the hearings is typical:

> Mr. Hinton: *Mr. Chairman, I think that you invited me here to ask me about my experiences in China. I came 3,000 miles at the taxpayers' expense. And it seems that this turns out that you are conducting an investigation about my sister and trying to get me to make statements against my sister.*

> The Chairman: *Mr. Hinton, we think it would be very valuable to this committee—this committee is charged with a duty. Now, you have knowledge, I feel, that you are not giving us. You said a while ago that you were a good, loyal American. Why do you not help this committee?*

> (Mr. Hinton confers with his counsel.)

> Mr. Hinton: *I am here to answer all proper questions, and that is all I will do.*

The testimony was covered in many national newspapers, including the *New York Times* and *Time* magazine, but the *Brattleboro Reformer* editorial page made it personal: "The colossal faith in the infallibility of [Hinton's] own judgment has helped exile his sister from her own country and has undoubtedly brought heartache to his mother and has created an unnecessary shadow on the institution which his mother founded."

In the case of the *Times*, William Hinton felt obliged to write a letter of correction: "That I defied the committee is correct. I believe that committees such as Jenner's are undermining the very foundations of our free society.... That I defied queries on China is untrue. They showed little interest in that subject. That I refused to say why I came home is also untrue. The question was never asked. It's a commonly known fact that I came home to settle down in the United States and start farming on my own."

Time painted William as "an idealist gone wrong": "What kind of American becomes a Communist or fellow traveler? Persistently both right and left tend to answer the question by referring to a type

Vt. Farmer Cites 5th Amendment When Questioned on Red Status

WASHINGTON, July 27 U⁒ — A⌐ Testimony brought out that Joan⌐ He said that in the summer of Vermont farmer who lived in China Hinton now in China worked on 1945 after spending one and a half

Brattleboro Reformer, July 28, 1950

that logically emerges from the writings of Marx: the pro-Communist is expected to be a poverty-driven, culturally disinherited rebel. But increasingly, the U.S. is aware of another type — not poverty-stricken, not rebellious by temperament, not disinherited by external economic forces but created by a subtle psychological rejection of the values upon which Western civilization has been built... . Last week, the committee faced such a man...a tall, raw-boned farmer-intellectual with gray flecks in his hair and credulity in his eyes."

Anxiety at the Putney School

It was the *Time* article, which also described the Putney School as "attracting the children of some of America's most alert and influential people," that caused the most anxiety in the school community. One concerned former student wrote to Carmelita Hinton: "It was indeed shocking for me to read an account of Bill's questioning by the Jenner Committee... . In light of this national publicity, I am wondering whether you plan to make any statement in regard to your position and that of the Putney School. I, for one, consider that Putney will remain under the shadow of suspicion until you have stated your opinion in this matter. It will be difficult for parents, alumnae, faculty and students to support the school and its ideals until you have cleared it and yourself of any connection with Communism (Fifth Amendment or otherwise)!"

An emergency meeting of the school's Executive Committee on July 27 had already raised the issue of such a statement. Ray Goodlatte was an English instructor who unofficially handled administrative duties during this summer, when Carmelita Hinton was at the family property in Cape Breton, Canada. Both the *Boston Herald* and the *Boston Globe* contacted Goodlatte after William Hinton's testimony, pressing him with questions about William's connection to the school. The chair of the Executive Committee, Richard Brett, proposed two alternatives:

> "1. Issue a statement declaring that William Hinton has no connection with the school and that his position is contrary to school policy. This must be carefully worded and done quickly, if at all.
>
> 2. Take no action of any kind unless the school is directly involved."

Brett continued, "At present time I have suggested to Goodlatte that he make no statement, that he report fully to Mrs H., and that he keep me informed of developments." The Putney School attorney, Osmer Fitts, concurred with Brett's reading:

> "I do not see that the school was sufficiently connected in the matter except by the reference to family connection, to warrant your first alternative, which as you say would be very difficult. In fact such a statement might lend credence to the belief that there is some direct connection with the school and of course statements issued later always serve to underscore the matter and bring it to the attention of a lot who may have missed it the first time. I would be hopeful that we could, in ways other than the public press, try to dispel the connection without in any way making it difficult for Mrs H. or compromising the broadmindedness of the school.... All in all I feel that the second alternative is the best one at least so far as the public press is concerned."

When William Hinton returned to Vermont after the Senate hearing, he and Brett had a chance to talk about the possible fallout for the school. It is clear from a letter William wrote to Brett shortly afterward that Brett had asked him to remain quiet for a while:

> From our talk I gather you strongly feel that the Putney School should stay out of controversy and thereby maintain immunity from attack so that it can continue to offer the kind of education

it has offered in the past. I think in this you assume that McCarthy and his colleagues will not attack the kind of education Putney has offered. Had the school not believed in these things (intellectual freedom and participation in the life of its community) it would have long ago degenerated into just another country club on a hill. In other words, the school has been involved in controversial issues because it is a live, vigorous place where personalities and ideas meet and clash. Such a place is a menace to McCarthy and all he stands for... there is no appeasing such a man or movement. You would have to start by screening the teachers, then the pupils, then the books in the library.

Carmelita Hinton refused to dissociate herself from her children's activities no matter how much heat she felt from the press, parents, and administrators. She defended William's work in China and later said about Joan: "It certainly made me mad when they called her a traitor.... I told them that she was having nothing to do with scientific research in China. She was in charge of 60,000 Peking ducks."

The formidable Mrs. H. had the support of most of the Putney School community in her defense of William and Joan. After the criticism in the aforementioned *Brattleboro Reformer* editorial, there was no more local press coverage of the issue. By the end of the summer the crisis had passed, and the new school year began without the cloud of controversy hanging over the campus.

Finally, *Fanshen*

William Hinton soon moved to Fleetwood, Pennsylvania, to a farm that Carmelita had purchased. His daughter Catherine theorizes that he was having trouble making a living due to FBI and press attention. Also, having managed the farm at Putney School during the middle years of the war in addition to the agricultural advising he had done in China with the UNRRA, he missed working on the land.

William also wished for a quiet place to begin work on his book about Long Bow Village, but the question of access to his voluminous notes still remained. According to his recollections years later, there had been a deal worked out with the Senate Committee on Internal Security: if he testified, he would have his notes returned. But in March 1956, when it became clear that this was not going to happen, he sued the Senate Committee. While the case wound its way through the courts over four years, he worked as a truck mechanic and a farmer, also giving periodic fundraising lectures (complete with Chinese dumplings).

When William won his case and retrieved the notes, he was finally able to devote himself to writing what came to be regarded as a classic, *Fanshen*. The meaning of that Chinese phrase, "to turn over," worked on two levels—as the literal turning of the soil and the political upending of the feudal system. He later observed that the denial of his notes for so many years, ironically, led to much better books. "In those five years, I traveled widely and talked to many American audiences and became attuned again to the American way of life which seemed so odd when I first came home.... By the time I did get the notes, I had developed an ability to talk to Americans on their level and the books that resulted were probably much better."

He was not surprised that, given the fearful times, *Fanshen* was turned down by every major publisher. It was finally published by the left-wing Monthly Review Press in 1966. After the book quickly sold out in hardcover, the paperback edition sold 200,000 copies. *Fanshen* was of keen interest to a new generation becoming radicalized and to an older, left-leaning group of Americans who had become disillusioned with the repressive Soviet model. In a 2009 appreciation published in *Counterpunch* magazine, John Walsh wrote: "As an antidote to the mainstream media's rush of misinformation and vitriol aimed at the Chinese revolution on its 60th anniversary, nothing is so effective as William Hinton's masterpiece.... The reader gets to know the participants, the peasants, by name and to witness their lives change forever as they take their destiny into their own hands for the first time in millennia."

William Hinton went on to lecture widely and publish several more books on China until his death in 2004. During the Cultural Revolution of the late 1960s, he became a crucial source for those trying to understand this volatile and confusing period. He returned to Long Bow Village in the late 1970s, a visit that led to a book sequel, *Shenfan,* which detailed what had changed in twenty years. His daughter Carma, a filmmaker, accompanied him on several return visits to Long Bow Village which resulted in her films *Small Happiness* and *All Under Heaven: Life in a Chinese Village.*

Joan Hinton and Sid Engst remained in China. After moving to Beijing for most of the duration of the Cultural Revolution, they returned to the countryside, farming in Shanxi Province until their deaths. In a 1996 interview with CNN, after nearly fifty years in China, Joan stated that they "never intended to stay in China so long, but were too caught up to leave." She and Sid supported the Cultural Revolution and thanks to their protected status as official Friends of the Chinese People were able to survive the unpredictable currents of that time. An unrepentant follower of Mao, Joan Hinton criticized the changes she and her husband witnessed in China after Premier Deng Xiaoping's economic reforms of the late 1970s. Joan said they "have watched their socialist dream fall apart" when much of China embraced capitalism. The 2010 *New York Times* obituary of Joan was headlined "Joan Hinton, Who Chose China Over Atom Bomb, Is Dead at 88."[2]

After leaving government work in the late 1940s, Jean Hinton Rosner became a teacher and advocate for causes ranging from peace in Central America to a host of environmental issues. She lived in Massachusetts for many years until her death at age 85. Though she had a much lower profile than her two siblings, her FBI file remained active until the 1970s, as mail from both William and Joan was monitored.

The FBI long continued to suspect the Hinton family of anti-American activities. In 1972, some at the bureau suspected (falsely, as it turned out) that members of the radical Weather Underground were hiding at the Hinton family compound at Sight Point, Cape Breton, Canada. Said the FBI report, "It is noted mem-

------

[2]Not all foreign supporters of Mao remained unscathed. Marni Rosner's in-laws, David and Isabel Crook, both longtime residents of China, were detained: David Crook for five years and Isabel Crook for three.

William Hinton and Joan Hinton Engst, China, 1993 (courtesy of Wikimedia Commons)

bers of the Hinton family and relatives over the years have been affiliated with a variety of subversive activities and espionage. This family actually might be described as representative of the 'Who's Who' of American Communism."

Carmelita Hinton herself remained politically active after her retirement from the Putney School in 1955. She became involved with the Women's International League for Peace and Freedom (WILPF) and visited China several times, staying for an entire year in 1971. In an interview with the *Boston Globe* shortly before her death in 1983, she said: "No, there's no use living on year after year just to live—to take a little nap and take a little nourishment and take a little walk. That's not life. If I can contribute, that's one thing.... To stop creating is to die."

The Putney School still thrives. On the home page of its website, Carmelita Hinton's first principles are still highlighted, including this one: "To combat prejudices caused by differences in economic, political, racial, and religious backgrounds; to strive for a world outlook, putting oneself in others' places, no matter how far away or how remote."

Senator Ralph Flanders (right) confronts Senator Joseph McCarthy and McCarthy's aide Roy Cohn, 1954 (Associated Press photo)

CHAPTER SIX / 1954

THE VERMONT PRESS AND JOSEPH McCARTHY'S DOWNFALL

When the longtime editor/publisher of the *Rutland Herald*, Robert Mitchell, spoke at the 1988 conference "Vermont in the McCarthy Era," he recalled a time in the early 1950s when Senator Joseph McCarthy commanded the news. "At that time it was automatic that anyone who opposed Senator McCarthy or others who exploited fears of subversion was likely to be charged with succumbing to the communist taint itself," Mitchell recalled. "During that period, the Herald published more editorials intending to debunk McCarthyism and the internal communist threat than were printed on any other subject."

And today? editorials should continue to concern Trump

Mitchell did not stop at anti-McCarthy editorials. The *Herald* also played a pivotal role in supporting the efforts of Senator Ralph Flanders in his battle with Senator Joseph McCarthy, a struggle that dominated the *Herald's* front pages from March through December 1954.

Senator Flanders, a Republican, might have seemed an unlikely figure to lead the opposition to Senator McCarthy of Wisconsin.

A machinist turned wealthy industrialist, Flanders was the epitome of the conservative, business-friendly Republican. He had served on many boards and blue-ribbon commissions, including a two-year stint as president of the Federal Reserve Bank in Boston. When Vermont senator Warren Austin was selected to become the first U.S. ambassador to the United Nations, Governor Mortimer Proctor appointed Flanders to fill out Austin's term. Flanders then won his first full term in 1948 at age sixty-eight, serving on the Finance Committee and the Armed Services Committee. He was generally considered far less liberal than Vermont's senior senator, George Aiken.

"The Four Horsemen of Calumny"

McCarthy had been elected to the Senate in 1946, but came into prominence only in February 1950 with his claim of communist infiltration in the State Department. The term "McCarthyism" followed not long after, coined by political cartoonist Herbert Block (known as Herblock) to denote exaggerated charges of subversion coupled with guilt-by-association attacks. By June 1950, Aiken had been so disturbed by McCarthy's tactics that he signed onto Maine senator Margaret Chase Smith's "Declaration of Conscience," the first official repudiation of McCarthy's anti-communist campaign. Smith's letter read in part, "I don't want to see the Republican Party ride to political victory on the Four Horsemen of Calumny: Fear, Ignorance, Bigotry and Smear." Smith noted later that the junior senator from Wisconsin had the Senate paralyzed with fear that he would act to defeat any senator who disagreed with him.

This apprehension was justified. In 1950, the Tydings Committee found McCarthy's charges of subversion in the State Department baseless, making Maryland's Democratic senator Millard Tydings a particular target of a McCarthy vendetta. That fall, McCarthy urged Tydings' Republican opponent in the senatorial election, John Marshall Butler, to publicize a doctored photo allegedly showing Tydings with former American Communist Party leader Earl Browder. Tydings' defeat in the election effectively ended his political career. Margaret Chase Smith herself was the intended victim

M'Carthy Doing His Best To Destroy Republican Party, Flanders Charges

Rutland Herald, July 16, 1954

in 1954 when McCarthy persuaded Richard Jones to run against her (unsuccessfully) in a Republican primary.

Four years after the "Declaration of Conscience," it was Flanders who ultimately took a more influential role than either Aiken or Smith in opposing McCarthy. What may have been a crucial factor for Flanders was his own view of the conservative/ liberal dichotomy. Flanders took an unusual approach for a self-described conservative businessman, acknowledging the need in society for a strong liberal voice. Liberalism, he said, represented the welfare of individual people. For him, conservatism was concerned with preserving institutions that serve the interests of people collectively. He began to fear that McCarthy's tactics, ruthlessly accusing liberals of being communist dupes, were ultimately weakening what Flanders felt was a necessary fight against communist influence worldwide. Flanders' experience on the Armed Services Committee also brought him into close contact with McCarthy, and he gradually wearied of McCarthy's self-promotion and disregard for facts.

McCarthy's much-ballyhooed 1953 investigation into communist subversion in the U.S. Army wound up focusing on one left-leaning dentist, Irving Peress, at Camp Kilmer, New Jersey. The Army countercharged that McCarthy and his staff (notably his assistant counsel, Roy Cohn) had arranged for preferential Army treatment for Private David Schine, a chief consultant to McCarthy's committee. Like some other Republicans, Flanders was concerned about the damage that McCarthy was doing to the Republican Party and sensed that President Eisenhower shared his concern.

Although the Army controversy tarnished McCarthy, many in public life still quaked at the thought of becoming one of his targets. He remained both a feared and admired figure in the press. Newspaper chains such as Hearst Publications were die-hard supporters; influential columnists such as Westbrook Pegler and George Sokolsky were scathing in their contempt for any anti-McCarthy sentiment. In Vermont this banner was carried by William Loeb, publisher of the *Burlington Daily News* and the *St. Albans Messenger,* who wrote frequent front-page diatribes against liberals and leftists and featured columns by strident conservatives Fulton Lewis Jr. and Victor Riesel.

Small-town editors and publishers like Robert Mitchell who opposed McCarthy were rare nationwide, though Mitchell had company in Vermont: Gerald McLaughlin of the *Springfield Reporter* and John Drysdale of the *White River Valley Herald,* among others. Mitchell had passionately defended some of McCarthy's intended victims; just four years earlier his *Rutland Herald* had taken the lead in investigating false charges that the Far East scholar Owen Lattimore had sold his Bethel property to benefit the Communist Party. (See Chapter Three.)

A Sunday interview in Springfield

But in early 1954, Mitchell was frustrated as he watched the weekly *Springfield Reporter* get exclusive interviews with Senator Flanders, a Springfield native who often returned home from the Capitol on weekends. What became known as the Army-McCarthy hearings, in which the Army's charges against Cohn and Schine were to be investigated, were scheduled to begin in April. There were rumblings that Flanders was preparing to criticize Senator McCarthy publicly.

An interview with the *Herald* was now of primary importance to Mitchell. His displeasure at getting scooped by the *Springfield Reporter* was conveyed to a young reporter, Kendall Wild, who covered Springfield for the *Herald.* Although Wild was later to become one of Vermont's outstanding journalists, at the time he was only twenty-five years old and eager to be in his boss' good graces. He used his Springfield contacts to find out when Flanders would be returning next. An interview was set for Sunday, March 8.

Speaking at the "Vermont in the McCarthy Era" conference in 1988, Wild recounted his experience. The current hot topic was a shocking event on March 1: an attempt by four Puerto Rican nationalists to assassinate members of Congress by firing randomly from the spectator's gallery. Flanders, as a member of the Armed Services Committee, had much to say about it. But eventually the conversation turned to McCarthy. "'Oh,' Flanders said, 'thanks for asking. I'm working on a speech that I'm going to give tomorrow when I go back to Washington.'" In 1988, Wild still regretted not asking Flanders for a peek at that speech, which seemed to be among the papers that Flanders was shuffling at his desk. "I think probably on the papers were the phrases that he used on the Senate floor the next day about McCarthy giving his war whoop and going out on the warpath and coming back with the scalp of a pink Army dentist." Instead, Flanders gave Wild the general drift, which left the young reporter "flabbergasted by his forthright criticism of this formidable national character."

As reported by Wild the next day, Flanders told Wild that McCarthy had "gone past his usefulness" and that there might be something done soon to "close this split in the Republicans' ranks." The story went on to quote Flanders saying that McCarthy "is using his methods to attract attraction to himself. Unfortunately, because of the kind of person he is, he can't seem to attract attention without embarrassing other people."

Flanders' Move To Oust McCarthy Sent to Committee

Rutland Herald, June 16, 1954

Rutland Herald, August 4, 1954

But there was more to that conversation, as Wild recalled years later: "One of my concerns was to protect this nice old guy from his carelessness and complete disregard to what would happen to him if he criticized McCarthy.... I thought then that going up against McCarthy was a not only very courageous but a foolish thing to do." The result was an article in which Wild "put in phrases that would show Flanders' reasonableness and not his foolishness."

Flanders' decision to take on McCarthy found enthusiastic support from one newspaper in particular, Wild's own *Rutland Herald*. With Wild's interview with Flanders on the front page, Mitchell's editorial that day read, "Senator Flanders made what may well be the 'understatement of the week' when he told a *Herald* representative that Senator McCarthy had 'outlived his usefulness'.... A lot of Americans, sincerely anti-Communist, have long been worried about the un-American methods and the divisive tactics of McCarthy."

Two days later, the Flanders speech on the Senate floor was front-page news across the country. The *Herald's* own headline read, "McCarthy Doing His Best to Destroy Republican Party, Flanders Charges." Although Flanders' audience included only a handful of senators and there were no television cameras or tape recorders, the coverage of the speech signaled a turning point in the McCarthy era.

Flanders' speech also emboldened other Republicans, nationally and in Vermont. The day that the *Rutland Herald* put the headline "Ike Terms Sen. Flanders Speech Against McCarthy a Real Service" on the front page, an additional story right below it was headlined "Disown McCarthy, Janeway Demands," quoting Republican National Committee member Edward Janeway as urging Republican leaders to rid themselves of an "embarrassing, self-made dilemma."

"Why do we bother with Joe?"

The *Herald* gave its support both in an editorial, "Sen. Flanders Speaks Out," and in a report on Flanders' speech from Washington correspondent Vonda Bergman that referred to McCarthyism as "the subject that so many seem to be running from these days." A few days later, Mitchell's periodic "Odds and Ends" column reported on the favorable press reaction in Vermont to Flanders' speech, quoting the *Barre Times* and the *Burlington Free Press*. The exception, wrote Mitchell, "was an anguished howl from the Loeb papers in Burlington and St. Albans whose owner, Bill Loeb, almost daily bows down and worships McCarthy."

Letters were largely in favor of Flanders, with "E.B." of Bethel writing in verse,

> Oh, why do we bother with Joe?
> Why don't we just let him go?
> Let him rant, let him rave
> Let him misbehave
> While we keep our minds on the show.

Flanders responded that week to one congratulatory note, "The trouble is that there are so many of you that (thanking everyone) has turned out to be practically impossible."

So similar to Trump [handwritten annotation]

As the Army-McCarthy hearings progressed throughout the spring of 1954, Flanders kept up his efforts to hold McCarthy to account. The immediate issue was McCarthy's refusal to appear before a Senate investigation that had explored his finances in 1952, but there was a growing sense of alarm among Republicans as McCarthy dominated the Army-McCarthy hearings with increasingly erratic behavior.

A turning point was reached on June 10, when McCarthy attacked Fred Fisher, a young lawyer in Army counsel Joseph Welch's firm, for a leftist past. This elicited Welch's famous rejoinder: "At long last, have you no decency?" "It was an outstanding example of McCarthy's unremitting willingness to destroy the reputation of an innocent bystander," Mitchell wrote on June 11. "When the hearings

Hugh Harley:
The Red Scare and the Labor Movement

Hugh Harley was a longtime labor activist. He worked for the International Labor Organization from 1937 to 1939 and then had a long association with the United Electrical, Radio and Machine Workers of America, first as an organizer (1940–1971) and then as director of organization (1971–1984). He was a guest speaker at the 1988 conference "Vermont in the McCarthy Era," where he made these remarks:

World War II was the greatest period of union-building in the United States. My union, United Electrical Workers, organized several shops in Vermont during the war. But with the end of the war came layoffs and cutbacks in hours, so the struggle for better living conditions came from unions like my own, the auto workers, and the steel and iron industries. Two million people hit the streets. Consternation occurred in the financial and industrial sectors of America.... It was known that the heads of U.S. Steel, General Electric and others met with Representative [Fred] Hartley and helped draft the 1947 Taft-Hartley law, which came to plague the labor movement during these years. The central part of this act that helped start the Red Scare was the non-Communist affidavit in the law [the law required union officers under the are ended, the principal damage to Sen. McCarthy's reputation will have been caused by the senator himself, if the trend of performance continues.... McCarthy has plenty of enemies, but he himself is far out in front of the list."

That same day, the *Herald* also ran the weekly "One Woman's Washington" report of Doris Fleeson of United Press International (one of the first women to have a syndicated political column): "That flower of evil which is McCarthyism bloomed in the Senate caucus room late Wednesday—rank and noxious, a fitting funeral blossom for the death of a republic.... An angry man (referring to Welch) cut it down and plunged it deep into the clear, cool waters of the New England conscience." When Flanders again attacked McCarthy

National Labor Relations Board's jurisdiction to submit anti-communist affidavits.] It was designed for a simple purpose: industry was aiming for a major goal, to split the unity of union people who had made gains, who had been building organizational strength and influence. The attacks began immediately in 1947, and UE was in the center of it—our members refused to sign the oath and we were basically expelled from union activity for two years. The Justice Department went after people they claimed took a false oath. The FBI tracked down people who refused to sign or who were suspected of signing falsely. The labor movement went from strength to being divided and weak. In my view McCarthyism and the House Un-American Activities Committee were tools in the campaign of corporate and financial interests.

In spite of the Red Scare, UE did not lose a single shop in Vermont, though our members were subjected to suspicion. I submit that there is a substantial tradition here to support a man's right to disagree as long as he's honest. In my experience of Vermont, it's not an accident that Ralph Flanders was the one who put the finishing touches on McCarthy. Flanders didn't want UE at the Jones and Lamson machine-tool plant [in Springfield, Vermont] that he ran, but when we presented our case to him, he knew we were right, and honesty forced him to do right by us.

the following day ("Flanders Rips M'C Anew," read the headline), McCarthy's response was, "I think they should get a man with a net and take him to a good quiet place."

On June 19, Flanders presented a motion to the Senate Rules Committee that McCarthy be stripped of his chairmanship of the Government Operations Committee. Republican Senate Majority Leader William Knowland denounced the motion and referred it to the Rules Committee, led by McCarthy supporter William Jenner.

"Contemptuous and Contumacious"

When that resolution was tabled, as Flanders had predicted, he then introduced a motion on July 30 to the full Senate that McCarthy be censured. Flanders, then seventy-four years old, was attacked as "senile" by both McCarthy and columnist George Sokolsky. Publisher William Loeb ran a front-page editorial urging readers to "wire the old gent.... Tell him to stop making himself, his state, and his country look ridiculous." Mitchell wrote a strong defense: "Vermonters generally know Senator Flanders and are not misled by such efforts to belittle the man who had the courage to oppose McCarthy."

On August 2, the Senate decided to refer the matter to a bipartisan select committee, headed by Arthur Watkins, Republican of Utah, and asked for a report before the end of the Eighty-third Congress in late 1954. Flanders was not hopeful about the outcome of this report, but on September 27, the Watkins Committee recommended censure, characterizing McCarthy's conduct as "contemptuous, contumacious, and denunciatory, without reason or justification and... obstructive to the legislature processes." The *Herald* editorial the following day concluded, "The report fully justifies Sen. Flanders and those of his colleagues who dared the McCarthy wrath by seeking to curb his intemperate, demagogic methods." Republicans succeeded in postponing the censure vote until after that November's election, when it was finally adopted by the full Congress on December 2 by a vote of 67–22.

Of the 67 "yeas," the vote among Republican senators was evenly split. One of those Republicans who voted for the censure was George Aiken. Despite his earlier support for the "Declaration of Conscience" in 1950, Aiken had taken a backseat to Flanders in the anti-McCarthy movement, choosing instead to devote his time to putting through as much as possible of President Eisenhower's program. Despite his own personal distaste for McCarthy, Aiken was troubled by such an extreme move as censure. He didn't discourage Flanders from going ahead with the resolution, but voted for it reluctantly. "I finally had to vote to censure Joe. I didn't want to, but I had to," he was quoted as saying.

The reaction among those anti-censure Republicans started the very next day. An unnamed Senate Republican was quoted in an Associated Press report as saying, "We will never forgive Sen. Flanders," adding that the Senate might lead some sort of action against Flanders in the future. What form of revenge this might take was revealed elsewhere in the *Herald* that day, as Senator William Jenner of Indiana accused Flanders of having contacts with two controversial figures, Harry Dexter White, a former Treasury Department official accused of being a Russian spy, and Owen Lattimore, a Far East specialist initially identified falsely by McCarthy as the head spy in the State Department.

These efforts to tar Flanders went nowhere and McCarthy's influence was dramatically diminished after the censure vote. Just a week after the vote, a *Herald* headline termed him "a man without friends." McCarthy's health suffered a steep decline (it is commonly accepted that alcoholism was a factor), and he died in 1957 toward the end of his second term. Flanders, at age seventy-eight in 1958, decided not to run for a third term.

In his memoir, *Senator from Vermont,* Flanders ended his chapter on McCarthy with the following: "In pursuit of headlines he had a masterly success, and the bullying and slurring provided acceptable journalistic material... . The press of our country must share in the blame for this unfortunate period in our history." However, the press in Vermont played its own crucial part in bringing Joseph McCarthy's career to an end.

Bernard "Bun" O'Shea, circa 1956 (courtesy of Clare [O'Shea] Bertrand)

BERNARD O'SHEA AND THE *SWANTON COURIER*

During the Red Scare years, Vermont remained a reliably one-party state, but within the Republican rubric, there were variations. The state's newspapers reflected these differing outlooks. For example, the *Rutland Herald* might be viewed as a sometime New Deal-supporting George Aiken brand of Republican, the *Burlington Free Press* a more conservative Eisenhower brand, and William Loeb's *Burlington Daily News* as a strident, pro-McCarthy example. As for the Democrats, one had to travel to Vermont's northwest corner, just a few miles from the Canadian border, to find an outspoken Democrat with a press platform. It was there that the eccentric and passionate Bernard "Bun" O'Shea held forth weekly in the pages of the *Swanton Courier*.

O'Shea was known in later years as a perennial Democratic candidate for statewide office and as a publisher in Enosburg Falls, Vermont, but it was during his years at the *Swanton Courier* that he first came to state-wide prominence. A native of Northampton,

Massachusetts, O'Shea was a reporter for the weekly *Berkshire Eagle* of Pittsfield, Massachusetts, when he and his wife, Sheila, bought the *Swanton Courier* from Jacob and Sarah Goodman in 1949. He became its publisher and Sheila the editor; as their son Kevin remembers, "My father was the dreamer, and my mother the driver."

The isolated and insular town of Swanton might have seemed like an unlikely destination for the worldly, well-educated O'Sheas (he was a graduate of Yale, she of Smith). Located in the farthest northwestern reaches of Vermont, Swanton is bordered on the west by Lake Champlain and Grand Isle County; the town limits extend northwest to the Canada–United States border within Missisquoi Bay, west of the town of Highgate. St. Albans, a larger town just minutes away, was home of the *Messenger,* the original newspaper of arch-conservative William Loeb's publishing realm.

The population of Swanton in 1950 was 3750, and at first glance, the *Swanton Courier* of the early 1950s resembles most small-town weeklies. Rarely does national news appear on the front page. Instead, you see features on farm bureau meetings, construction projects, 4-H club events, and local controversies. But open the paper to the editorial page and you will encounter passionate opinion and wide-ranging interest in national and international events, with a special emphasis on world peace and civil liberties. The previous owners had often written about international affairs. In Jacob Goodman's farewell message, he writes, "I have come to the conclusion that there is more individual morality as evidenced here in Swanton, or for that matter in any community, than there is in the collective morality of all governments.... . Individuals would never dream of sharpening arms to kill a neighbor."

"To inform the public…"

In their very first editorial, the O'Sheas elaborated on this message: "The editors will be concerned with this community, not to the exclusion of a country upon which it depends, or to the exclusion of a world in which it must live at peace in order to survive, but as the focal point of our human interests." Soon the paper's masthead bore the motto, "The Constant Aim of this Newspaper is to inform

Sheila and Bernard O'Shea, shortly after their marriage.
(Courtesy of Clare [O'Shea] Bertrand)

the public honestly and intelligently." With frequent editorials on disarmament and world peace, the O'Sheas quickly established the *Courier* as a liberal counterweight to the *St. Albans Messenger.* [1]

Both the O'Sheas had been profoundly affected by their World War II experiences. They each served in the Navy, Bernard commanding a submarine chaser in the Pacific, and Sheila working in Washington, D.C., as a code breaker. According to the O'Sheas' son Chris, they both returned from the war determined pacifists and soon became involved with the American Society of Friends (Quakers). O'Shea evoked his wartime experience in a 1954 editorial shortly after an atomic bomb test on the island of Eniwetok:

------

[1]Although Sheila O'Shea was the editor of the paper as a whole, the editorials themselves became her husband's domain, with an occasional contribution from Sheila. A prescient editorial of hers from 1952 discusses the significance of local sightings of Confederate flags, and another in 1953 commended the controversial studies of sexuality by Dr. Alfred Kinsey. "Delinquency and depravity existed long before Dr. Kinsey and will continue to until we have a proper understanding of the causes behind the breakdown in our morals," Sheila O'Shea wrote. "Whatever contributes to that understanding is good, and we believe Dr. Kinsey's years of research have a definite contribution to make."

NEW EDITORS TAKE OVER COURIER TODAY

This week The Courier was sold by Mr. and Mrs. J. A. Goodman to Mr. and Mrs. Bernard G. O'Shea of Canaan, N.Y. The new owners assume the editorship of the newspaper with this edition.

Both Mr. and Mrs. O'Shea will manage and edit the publication. Mr. O'Shea has spent the years since World War II in newspaper and advertising work. Most recently he was a reporter for the Berkshire Evening Eagle of Pittsfield, Mass. Before entering the newspaper business Mr. O'Shea taught at Columbia University in New York City. During the war he was commanding officer of a Navy submarine chaser in the Pacific.

The new editor is a native of Northampton, Mass. He is a graduate of Yale University and Deerfield Academy.

Mrs. O'Shea is the former Sheila Casey of Rouses Point, N.Y., the daughter of Mr. and Mrs. W. Rossiter Casey of that neighboring town. Mrs. O'Shea is a graduate of The Low-Heywood School in Connecticut, and Smith College. During the war she served as a Lt. (jg) in the WAVES in Washington, D.C. The O'Sheas have two sons, Kevin Casey, 3 years, and Christopher Wolfe, four months. The family will occupy the apartment in The Courier building this winter.

Mr. and Mrs Goodman will leave Swanton about November 1, after ten and one half years of managing The Courier. The former editors will make their new home in Boston where Mr. Goodman will write. The Goodmans also expect to travel during the next year. Mr. Goodman

Swanton Courier, October 14, 1949

"More than 10 years ago, I walked onto the blood-stained coral island called Eniwetok. I used to swim under water with water-tight glasses on to better observe the coral formations, the sea vegetation, and the beautifully colored and oddly-shaped fish that would swim by my eyes. I was thinking of all this while looking at pictures of the H-bomb blast. The island I describe is now only a black crater in the sea. A black hole that even a dozen Pentagon buildings wouldn't fill. The little island is gone—blasted out of the Pacific.... I'll be thinking about this as I swim underwater in Lake Champlain too."

Another editorial, this one from 1951, commemorated the dropping of the atomic bomb on Nagasaki, Japan, with a reprint from a book by Japanese children, "Living Under the Atom-Cloud." O'Shea introduced the piece by saying, "Since those days six years ago, many have grown calloused to atomic warfare. Forgetting all humanity, these voices are raised asking that we 'solve' our international disputes with a rain of atomic bombs."

"A symptom of deeper troubles..."

That 1951 editorial was one of many that used books, articles, and public talks as a starting point for columns with a strong international perspective. A sample of those who inspired O'Shea's editorials reads like a list of left-liberal luminaries of the time: *Saturday Review of Literature* editor Norman Cousins; Robert Hutchins, outspoken president of the University of Chicago; Stringfellow Barr, president of St. John's College and a leader in progressive education; radical peace activist Dorothy Day, editor of *The Catholic Worker*; and the secretary-emeritus of the pacifist Fellowship of Reconciliation, A.J. Muste.

Muste's words especially struck a chord in Bernard O'Shea (He and Sheila were both members of the Fellowship of Reconciliation). He agreed with Muste's thesis that McCarthyism was "only a symptom of deeper troubles of tensions, conflict, violence, and fears we are trying manfully to conquer in today's revolutionary world." It was a theme that O'Shea returned to time and again, in an idiosyncratic and lively style. A sample editorial from 1951 reads, "One of the most serious victims of the Cold War is the tradition of protest which has been such a great part of American intellectualism. Today in the miasma of McCarthyism, Orthodoxy has become the great god…and false idol. The protesting but loyal American has learned that by speaking out he is immediately suspect."

From his remote perch in Swanton, the well-informed O'Shea saw the dangers that the anti-communist crusade was bringing to other parts of the world. In the summer of 1954, a liberal coalition government in Guatemala was under attack by rebels. It later became public knowledge that this was a coup sponsored by the Central Intelligence Agency, but O'Shea was able to discern events in Guatemala as they were happening. His editorial, with characteristically convoluted phrasing, blamed the United Fruit Company directly: "United Fruit bears a heavy responsibility not only because it has apparently been financing the invading rebels, but because it skimmed off the banana cream while allowing conditions to exist in this barefoot republic which brought on the "New Deal" reform government which encouraged communists in its coalition… . Further, reports indicating that Allen Dulles, head of the CIA, has been working with United Fruit in trying to overthrow the Guatemalan government, makes the matter even more intriguing."

Although O'Shea inveighed often against the rising tide of McCarthyism nationally, events in Vermont occupied his attention from the start. One of his first editorials took Vermont's Republican congressman, Charles Plumley, to task for a particularly bellicose speech: "If Mr. Plumley thinks our present leaders can find no basis for any kind of lasting agreements with the Eastern world he should tell us why he thinks this. And if he thinks it is a 'certainty and sooner than most of us think' at that, then he should tell us why mass destruction and killing is preferable to making the compromises necessary for international agreements."

Plumley was again O'Shea's target when the retiring congressman charged that Vermont's history textbooks needed to be purged of communist indoctrination. While several Vermont newspapers challenged Plumley to show them proof, O'Shea thought even this pushback was not enough. "In our opinion such an investigation,

Swanton Courier, July 26, 1951

even if it turned up as bona fide, [purging the 10 communist teachers] that the FBI says are hiding in the Vermont woodwork, would not be worth the real damage it would do to the democratic goals of our educators." O'Shea concluded that "Mr. Plumley knows that the time-tested sure-fire way to cow the educators and intimidate the entire Vermont educational system is to charge communist infiltration in the schools.... We hope Vermont teachers stand firm against the politician and others who would judge them. If they do not they only invite the destruction of their academic freedoms." When Plumley tried once more, in 1953, to have a bill introduced in the legislature to oversee content of Vermont's history textbooks, O'Shea turned a whole page over to reprinting the opinions of other editors around the state. Nine editorial writers, from the *Addison Independent* to the *Woodstock Standard,* reacted to Plumley's proposal with outrage and scorn. "Go back to your rocking chair, Uncle Charlie," concluded one.

Swanton Courier, July 9, 1953

A defense of Novikoff

In April 1953, O'Shea became the only editorial writer in Vermont to offer an outspoken defense of University of Vermont professor Alex Novikoff when Novikoff was threatened with dismissal for his political views (see Chapter Four). O'Shea not only argued for Novikoff's retention but also offered an eloquent defense of free thought in academia and beyond.

While other editorialists (notably in the *Burlington Free Press* and *Burlington Daily News*) stated that Novikoff's use of the Fifth Amendment before a Senate Committee was sufficient grounds for dismissal, O'Shea thought otherwise. "An alarming development in the Novikoff case has been the irresponsible charges of 'Americanism' thrown about," he wrote in the spring of 1953. "Statements that those who still believed in the Fifth Amendment are somehow not 'good Americans' have been too widespread, propagated by many people who should know better." He added, "Actually the Novikoff incident is only another example of many on the wide assault on traditional American principles."

O'Shea strongly condemned the decision of the University of Vermont to overturn a 5-1 committee decision to retain Novikoff. "It was fear of loss of state funds, and public attacks from Reynolds (Milo Reynolds, editor of the *Suburban List*) and Loeb (William Loeb, publisher of the *St. Albans Messenger* and the *Burlington Daily News*) that caused the trustees to take an action... that few of them as individuals really believe." After Novikoff's eventual dismissal, O'Shea turned philosophical: "Members of the teaching profession are learning that 'academic freedom' has lost its meaning.... This is a time of great change and few trustees today are going to defend teachers' freedom for them."

In March 1954, O'Shea attacked then state Attorney General Elliott Barber for proposing loyalty oaths for state employees. "Barber is benighted indeed if he thinks that copying the confusion in Washington is going to help us in Montpelier. Loyalty in a family, church or state is an intangible combination of individual conscience, faith and trust of men and women in each other. You can't get it by making people sign a piece of paper." Calling loyalty oaths "a symptom of our patriotic fears," O'Shea concluded the long editorial with a pointed allusion to the New Hampshire Attorney General Louis Wyman, a strident anti-Communist leading his own investigations. O'Shea's suggestion was to "look around us in the world—beyond New Hampshire and Washington, D.C. What are the countries that have demanded loyalty oaths? Germany, Russia, Yugoslavia, Spain. Are these the countries Americans and Vermonters now want to imitate?"

In the summer of 1954, the nation was riveted by the Army-McCarthy hearings, which many historians point to as the act of hubris that brought McCarthy down. O'Shea wrote, "We hope the hearings have shown us how valuable are our constitutional separation of powers. Certainly if we allow a demagogue to trample down these safeguards, we do not deserve the democracy our forefathers willed us...."

The hearings gave impetus to Vermont senator Ralph Flanders' own efforts to censure McCarthy. Like most Vermont editors,

O'Shea was firmly behind Flanders; the controversy elicited some of O'Shea's most fervent writing. Calling McCarthy "a vilifier of decent men," he praised Flanders: "Flanders' action is a courageous move to keep the GOP a responsible instrument in American political life. This is a deep dispute between enlightened conservatives and the radical reactionaries led by McCarthy." Once again saving his sharpest barbs for William Loeb, he went on: "We are pleased to see so many Vermont papers supporting Flanders—all have laid aside differences they may have with the Senator to support him in this showdown.... People in the Northwestern Vermont who rely on the *Burlington Free Press* and the Loeb papers for their daily news diet should not get the mistaken impression that the majority of the press and readers are with McCarthy."

Throughout the years, the O'Sheas' *Courier* and Loeb's *St. Albans Messenger* attacked each other with abandon. When Loeb accused Senator Flanders of selling machinery to the Soviet Union (in his role as a Springfield industrialist), the O'Sheas put Flanders' rebuttal on the front page, with the headline "Flanders Answers Radical Attacks." In one delicious piece of irony, a few days after Loeb attacked O'Shea as "a do-gooder who would take in a frozen rattlesnake and warm it by the hearth," the linotype at Loeb's St. Albans plant broke down, and some of the *Courier*'s staff were called on for help fixing it. Said O'Shea, "Some people still consider the term 'do-gooder' a slur, but fortunately for our country, most of us do not."

"Drive-em-underground and dig-em-up-again"

One of O'Shea's strongest editorials of this era was one headlined, "Poor Politicians Pastime," which began, "Our policy of mining gold and then building Fort Knox to put it in the ground again is based on securing the monetary system. Our policy of driving the Communists underground and then 'investigating' them out into the light of public display again is founded on a kind of security, although few can agree what this security is.... This conversion of communism from a political philosophy and economic system to a 'conspiracy' in the nation, has in the process just about destroyed all sane study of its real functions and purposes in the great part of the world where it is now accepted and become all-powerful."

In the same editorial, O'Shea took a swipe at both ex-Congressman Plumley ("Vermont's gift to Washington hysteria for many years, whose requests for investigations are always turned down by our sane and sober legislators.") and New Hampshire's Attorney General Louis Wyman, who has "gone in for this drive-em-underground and dig-em-up-again game with the communists." O'Shea then wondered about the difference between New Hampshire and Vermont: "Why does one community do these things and another not? Much seems to lie in the spirit as well as the tradition of the society. Once a people get hysterical it is difficult to stop the stampede. And it only seems to take a few strong demagogues."

There was some pushback against the O'Sheas from more conservative Swanton locals. Chris O'Shea remembers his mother "dragging out her service record and telling a guy, 'I'm just as good an American as you are.'" Kevin O'Shea wonders how many people

THE BIG SPLIT

Ralph Flanders represents in Congress the Eisenhower kind of Republican: "In all things which deal with people, be liberal, be human . . . with the people's money or their form of government, be conservative." His voting record, his actions since becoming a Senator, show this.

Joe McCarthy is the reverse. He's the leader of the radical reactionaries in the Republican party. His campaign is based on suppression, distrust, destructive cynicism. Their aim is first the capture of the GOP and the U.S. government, then the capture of Asia. He has considerable support in the press, some smooth, informed, polite like David Lawrence, others more crude like Fulton Lewis Jr.

Swanton Courier, June 24, 1954

did read the editorials, and how many only preferred to learn what was happening locally. "I could never figure out who my father's intended audience was," he said recently.

But an article in a 1952 issue of *Fellowship* (the magazine of the Fellowship of Reconciliation) painted a rosier picture of the local situation:

> "The O'Sheas recognize their fellow Vermonters as clear-thinking, alert and independent individuals most of them are, and talk to them through the columns of paper in the reasonable, adult tone suitable for conversation among equals. It is probably this attitude as much as anything that has made it possible for Bun and Sheila, in three short years, to put so large dent in the tired old myth that Vermonters will not accept to their friendship and counsels any 'outlander' who has not lived in the state at least half his life."

"He loved getting out and meeting people"

Starting in 1956, at age 37, O'Shea took on the balancing act of being both a publisher and a political candidate. He amazed family, friends, and political observers by launching a quixotic campaign against the Republican incumbent George Aiken, already a Vermont icon, in the race for senator after no Democrat stepped forward. At that year's state Democratic convention, he called the Republican Party, "a mossy, moldy party, organized for the few." He lost overwhelmingly that year, by 48,000 votes. A few years later, he responded to Representative William Meyer's pro-disarmament positions, and became a trusted advisor on Meyer's 1960 unsuccessful re-election campaign (see Chapter Nine for more on that campaign). During the next two decades, he ran and lost three races for Congress and one for governor. "He just loved getting out and meeting people," said longtime friend and employee Nat Worman. "He was an astonishingly brave, cool, smart person."

In the late 1950s, O'Shea moved his operations to Enosburg Falls, Vermont. Under the heading of the *County Courier,* the *Swanton Courier* joined the *Enosburg Standard,* the *Richford Gazette* and the *St. Albans Leader.* He served for a time as director and vice-president of the Vermont Council on World Affairs, and as peace education secretary of the American Friends Service Committee of New England, all the while writing stinging editorials against the Vietnam War. In the spirit of the times, he also hired several young writers who arrived in Vermont as part of the "back-to-the-land" movement. One of those budding journalists, Roy Towlen, recalls that a fellow recruit was Bernie Sanders, who, after a short stint at the paper, wrote a letter of resignation, "exasperated by the chaotic atmosphere at the *Courier*."

But one person's chaos is another person's magic, which is how another recruit, Tyrone Shaw, described his time at the *Courier*. "I couldn't have asked for a better introduction to journalism," said Shaw. "Bun was seemingly unperturbed by any negative reactions to his stories.... He was deeply courageous and was humble and reticent about that courage." Nat Worman added that from his vantage point he never considered Bun as a traditional "boss": "He didn't tell you to do something. Instead he waited till you figured out it needed to be done."

O'Shea had turned over operations of the papers to his son, Chris, but was still active politically when he died in New York City in 1988 after suffering a heart attack while addressing an international conference sponsored by the anti-war group Mobilization for Survival.

Robin Lloyd, a peace activist of the younger generation, recalls O'Shea's "warm and open" presence at Quaker meetings. He was remembered by his friend David Hutchinson shortly after his death in the *St. Albans Messenger:* "Bun had that rarest of abilities, the capacity to remind people of their best qualities, their noblest ideals.... His unwavering respect for people, his value of friendship over belief, and his own personal courage and convictions were the tools he used best."

Today the bound copies of the *Courier* from 1949-1956 rest in the Swanton Historical Society. Leafing through the weekly papers, one can feel in the presence of a remarkable, ardent journalist whose heartfelt editorials belie the stereotypical concept of the 1950s as an era marked by acquiescence.

University of New Hampshire professor Gwynne Harris Daggett
with student, circa 1953 (courtesy of Priscilla Daggett)

CHAPTER EIGHT / 1951–1958

MEANWHILE, ACROSS THE CONNECTICUT RIVER...

A recent *New York Times* article referred to Vermont and New Hampshire as "New England's unidentical twins," while another observer termed the two states "geographic twins, but cultural aliens." Long before anyone thought to divide our country into red and blue, observers have long noted the differences between the two states.

Some point to Vermont's longstanding libertarian streak. While Vermont outlawed slavery in 1777, it wasn't until 1857 that New Hampshire—the "Live Free or Die" state—passed a law which declared, "No person, because of descent, should be disqualified from becoming a citizen of the state." In fact, Portsmouth, New Hampshire was a particularly attractive landing spot for slavers, as New Hampshire didn't charge a tariff for importing slaves, who might then be smuggled into other colonies.

Others say that geology is destiny. In 1959, political scientist Duane Lockard wrote, "The scouring glaciers were kinder to the Vermont hillsides than to New Hampshire." In 1900, Vermont's economy was among the most agriculturally based of any of the fifty states while New Hampshire's was among the least. Industry gave rise to larger cities in New Hampshire; one result, in the view of Paul Sweezy, a Marxist economist, part-time New Hampshire resident, and, as we shall see, target of New Hampshire's Red Scare, was a manufacturing economy structured on traditional capitalist lines with great inequities between owners and workers.

Journalist Joe Sherman points to the Québécois influence in northern Vermont. Unlike the emigres who became mill workers in New Hampshire, Sherman noted the Québécois who settled in northern Vermont were integrated into both the agricultural economy and into politics.

Higley Hill:
A Camp for "Young Progressives"

During the Red Scare years, Vermont had a number of summer camps whose clientele included children of blacklisted parents. Paul Heller discussed one of these camps, Higley Hill, in a 2016 article for the Barre-Montpelier Times Argus.

"The 4-H Lassies met Saturday afternoon with Miss Caroline White at the home of Mrs. Max Granich. Miss Shirley Cole demonstrated sewing on bias binding. Miss Marie Moore gave a demonstration of buffet decoration. Refreshments were served by Mrs. Granich."

The above item from the North Adams Transcript of Feb. 15, 1952, suggests a bucolic scene from mid-20th century America, with girls and women gathering at a routine meeting of a youth group that extolled fundamental agrarian values. In a most unlikely scenario, however, the hostess of this event, Mrs. Grace Granich, had the month before been denounced by the House Un-American Activities Committee "as a menace to the security of the United States." The *Boston Daily Record* described her appearance as she "took the fifth": "A graying and grandmotherly appearing figure, Mrs. Granich refused to answer all questions about her activities since 1930 on grounds

Duane Lockard theorized that another consequence of increased industry and more diverse immigration to New Hampshire was that "the greater heterogeneity made its politics more tempestuous." The events that unfolded in New Hampshire during the 1950s were indeed "tempestuous." Though both Vermont and New Hampshire were considered die-hard Republican strongholds at the time, there was a significant difference in how each state reacted to the national political climate of the 1950s.

During the Red Scare years, there were three powerful people who shaped much of the public opinion in New Hampshire, creating an atmosphere that was more heated than Vermont. The first was New Hampshire's U.S. senator H. Styles Bridges, who was far

that to answer might tend to incriminate her. Despite threats of contempt citations, the Granichs claimed their constitutional privilege against being required to give self-incriminating testimony."

Max and Grace Granich had led interesting lives as functionaries of the United States Communist Party, and Higley Hill, their Wilmington, Vermont, summer camp offered a quiet refuge for children from the city—children whose parents were the target of Joseph McCarthy and right-wing red-baiters. Alex Levy offered this remembrance in 2011: "Often, with their parents in jail and facing abuse and ostracism at school and in their neighborhoods, the children of the Old Left needed to get away, preferably to the country in the summer; they needed shelter and unconditional love, and this was provided by Max and Grace Granich. That neither of them had much experience working with children made no difference. They provided a summer home in which American ideals of tolerance, the virtue of physical labor, and inclusiveness were lived. However, Grace had little tolerance for competitive games, fancy makeup, smoking or 'wild' music. Of course, as in all summer camps, some kids were not overly happy. But on the whole, Higley Hill was a haven."

During that period, the farm was frequently visited by FBI agents and investigators from HUAC, and they were uniformly treated with courtesy and told nothing whatsoever. The neighbors knew of these visits and were always supportive of the Granichs.

more conservative than Vermont's Republican senators George Aiken and Ralph Flanders. Bridges was elected Governor in New Hampshire in 1934, then won a Senate seat in 1937, soon becoming the most influential politician in the state. The journalist John Gunther termed Bridges "an aggressive reactionary on most issues...pertinaciously engaged in a continual running fight with the C.I.O. (Congress of Industrial Organizations, a left-leaning labor confederation), the Roosevelt family, and the U.S.S.R." He was also one of the forces behind the so-called "Lavender Scare" of the early 1950s, which purged hundreds of homosexuals from the State Department and other government agencies.

Another influential person was publisher William Loeb, who bought the *Manchester Union-Leader* in 1949 and used it (as he had used his two Vermont papers, the *Burlington Free Press* and *Burlington Daily News*) as a platform for his extreme anti-communist views. New Hampshire's only statewide paper, the *Union-Leader* dominated the New Hampshire political scene, with a circulation greater than all other state dailies combined (Vermont, by contrast, had no one paper of such outsized influence). Phil Nicoloff, a University of New Hampshire English professor at the time, recalled, "It was a political necessity in the state to have William Loeb on your side and to be seen as someone who could rout out dangerous subversives."

Perhaps the most telling difference in the experience of the two states was that the anti-communist fervor of the times had official state backing in New Hampshire, and this is where New Hampshire's Attorney General Louis C. Wyman exerted his influence. In 1952, the legislature (known as the General Court) passed the Subversive Activities Act, which made it a felony to teach or advocate "doctrines tending toward the overthrow of government by force." In 1953, the legislature took another step, giving Wyman the authority to conduct an investigation into whether the University of New Hampshire or any tax-supported institution engaged in such "subversive activities." As Duane Lockard observed, "The legislature authorized a fire-breathing attorney general (a protégé of Senator Bridges) to search out subversion instead of laughing the proposition out of court as the Vermonters had done."

VOLUME NO. 44 ISSUE 16   UNIVERSITY OF NEW HAMPSHIRE, DURHAM, N. H. — May 27, 1954   PRICE — SEVEN

DAGGETT WON'T ANSWER, WYMAN PRESSES CONTEMPT PROCEEDINGS

University of New Hampshire newspaper *The New Hampshire*, May 27, 1954

Between the years 1953 and 1959, Wyman investigated 131 people, taking advantage of his license to target dissenting academics. Although several Dartmouth professors, including Alexander Laing and Vilhjalmur Stefansson (see Chapter Three for more on Stefansson), were harassed by Wyman, his main target was the state-financed University of New Hampshire. Humanities professor Gwynne Harris Daggett was singled out both for his off-campus activism (he had been a state organizer for the Henry Wallace presidential campaign in 1948) and for his classroom speaker list, which included Paul Sweezy. Sweezy was an obvious target, as both a vocal supporter of Henry Wallace and as one of the co-founders of the Marxist publication *Monthly Review*. He and Daggett were called before Wyman's panel to produce the notes for his lecture to Daggett's class, which would serve as ostensible proof of "advocating subversive doctrines."

Daggett attacked Wyman's investigating committee in a statement to the college community: "However it is to be handled, it is apparently to be an inquisition into the political opinions and affiliations of individual citizens. Such an inquiry, it seems to me, is contrary to both the ideals and methods of democracy. We cannot save democracy in general by destroying it in particular."

Although both Sweezy and Daggett answered most questions, they refused to give any information that they felt went beyond the scope of Wyman's authority. Wyman successfully argued before the New Hampshire Supreme Court that the two must answer questions about their Progressive Party activities and about Sweezy's lecture to the Daggett's humanities class.

As one student pointed out in the University of New Hampshire newspaper, the authorities could have obtained the information they needed about the lecture from any student's notes. But rather than risk uncertainty about his teaching position and the expense of an appeal to the higher courts, Daggett ultimately turned over what he called a "reconstructed text" of Sweezy's lecture, and answered questions about his Progressive Party involvement. He continued to teach his popular humanities class until his death in 1969. As Daggett's daughter Priscilla Daggett recalls, "My father was exonerated because of his popularity as a teacher and because the University, to their everlasting credit, defended him."

Sweezy and his attorney, Professor Thomas Emerson of Yale Law School, decided on a more defiant strategy: not answering certain questions, with an eye towards an appeal. Sweezy was convicted of contempt with a three-year jail sentence. "I knew I'd be found guilty, so we immediately appealed." The decision was upheld by the New Hampshire State Supreme Court. But in 1957, the United States Supreme Court ruled in Sweezy's favor by a 6-2 margin. Earl Warren's majority opinion stated: "Teachers and students must always remain free to inquire, to study and to evaluate, to gain new maturity and understanding; otherwise our civilization will stagnate and die."

Sweezy was a guest at the 1988 conference, "Vermont in the McCarthy Era." There he spoke of the atmosphere in his small town of Wilton, New Hampshire, where his family had summered since 1914. "No one who knew us believed we were dangerous radicals.... The town was tolerant, but a supportive attorney warned me that someone was taking license plate numbers in front of our house." Sweezy continued, "There are always good people who don't fall for terror tactics, and believe me, some people felt terrorized.... It's hard to believe how far it went until you experienced it."

Reflecting on his battle with Wyman and the malicious attacks by Loeb, Sweezy recalled, "Wyman didn't have much to work with.... The state had no tradition of radical politics or political movements, so the problem of working up a Red Scare was not an easy one."

Another of Wyman and Loeb's targets was the Reverend Willard Uphaus, who with his wife, Ola Hawkins Uphaus, directed the interfaith conference center in Conway, New Hampshire, known as the World Fellowship Center. Uphaus had been an outspoken pacifist and before moving to New Hampshire had directed the left-wing National Religion and Labor Foundation for twenty years. In 1953 the couple had barely finished their first year at the center when they learned that they were on Loeb and Wyman's radar (The *Union-Leader*'s headline was "Pro-Red Takes Over New Hampshire Fellowship Group"). Wyman soon demanded their membership rolls, and Uphaus refused.

The case dragged on for five years until November 14, 1958, when the United States Supreme Court ruled by a 5-4 margin that given the power granted Wyman by the Legislature, the attorney general could force Uphaus to produce the guest list or prosecute him. Rather than surrender the membership list, Uphaus chose jail. On the day the sixty-nine-year-old Uphaus was led away to

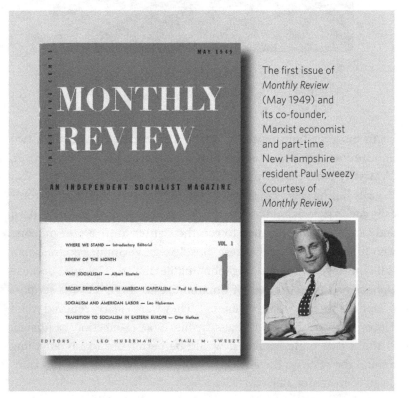

The first issue of *Monthly Review* (May 1949) and its co-founder, Marxist economist and part-time New Hampshire resident Paul Sweezy (courtesy of *Monthly Review*)

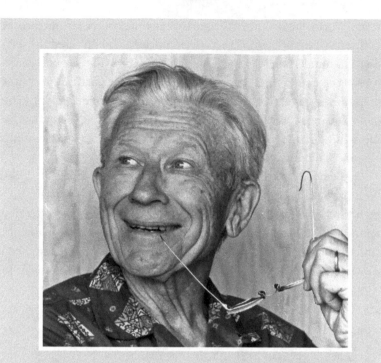

Reverend Willard Uphaus in later years (courtesy World Fellowship Center)

begin his year-long sentence at the Merrimack County Jail, two hundred supporters cheered him on, singing his favorite hymn, "A Mighty Fortress is Our God."

His jailing was a cause célèbre in the national media, and ironically gave a significant boost to the World Fellowship Center. Willard and Ola Uphaus continued to run the Center until 1969. Someone who followed the Uphaus case closely was Vermont congressman William Meyer, who kept a large clipping file labeled, "Uphaus." Because Uphaus had been accused of Communist leanings, Meyer's support of Uphaus worried some of his staff. They were clearly relieved when Meyer did not discuss Uphaus in his 1960 re-election campaign. "I think that quite frankly it would be better not to say anything around the state on the subject," wrote one advisor to Meyer's campaign coordinator, Bernard O'Shea.

A final note: when Paul Sweezy was invited to address the 1988 conference about his experiences in New Hampshire, we organizers discovered that the past was far from dead and buried. John McClaughry, a Vermont Historical Society member and soon to become a well-known Republican state senator and conservative political commentator, wrote to the Historical Society, "I wonder how it was decided to invite this well-known Marxist propagandist to a scholarly conference.... What does the Society expect this person to contribute to what I presume is intended to be a dispassionate scholarly analysis?....In short, is this scholarship or a propaganda session?" Michael Sherman, then the VHS director, responded, "Mr. Sweezy was asked to speak not on Marxism or his own political philosophy, but on his experience in the 1950s living in New Hampshire where, by legislative resolution, an individual could be charged with contempt for refusing to answer questions about political associations and activities.... As you know, Vermont had no such law."

William H. Meyer of West Rupert, Vermont (courtesy of University of Vermont Special Collections)

CHAPTER NINE / 1958–1960

THE CONGRESSIONAL CAMPAIGNS OF WILLIAM H. MEYER

Trace the roots of Bernie Sanders' improbable rise in Vermont and one is inescapably led to William H. Meyer, an unassuming forester from the tiny hamlet of West Rupert who reshaped Vermont's political landscape during the waning days of the Red Scare.

Ask most Vermonters today to identify Meyer and you're likely met with puzzled looks. Vermont historians and political veterans, however, know Meyer as the 1958 Democratic candidate who wrested the Vermont seat in the U.S. House of Representatives from Republican control after 104 years. Progressives in Vermont with long memories know of him as an outspoken liberal who espoused nuclear disarmament, critiqued militarism, and advocated for the recognition of "Red" China. In 1970, retired from mainstream electoral politics, Meyer co-founded (along with Bernie Sanders and others) the Liberty Union Party.

"Unusual warmth and sincerity"

Meyer, a Philadelphia native, graduated from the School of Agriculture at Penn State and worked as a forester for the federal government. Enamored of the Vermont landscape and pace of life, he soon requested a transfer to Vermont and settled with his wife, Bertha, in West Rupert, a hamlet about 25 miles north of Bennington. His activities in the community included stints as a volunteer fireman, a 4-H club and Boy Scout leader, a member of the Sportsmen's Club, and the editor of a small statewide publication called *Wildlife*.

Meyer's path to Congress was an extremely unlikely one. His residence in West Rupert placed him outside the two centers of the Vermont Democratic Party, Rutland and Burlington. Electoral experience prior to Meyer's historic 1958 congressional race was a losing run for the Vermont House two years earlier. Such was his party profile that as the Democratic congressional candidate two years later he attended a statewide party meeting in Burlington and was unrecognized.

His initial idea was to run for the U.S. Senate. Meyer's son Karl remembers accompanying his father to nearby Salem, New York to post the press release announcing his bid. Meyer astutely crossed the border because he was not prepared to have the local postmaster in West Rupert question him or gossip to townspeople before his announcement was published statewide. But a month later, party leaders—fearing the prospect of a primary fight with veteran Burlington Democrat Fred Fayette—persuaded him to try for the House instead, a race yet to have a Democratic candidate. Although Meyer received nominal support from the Democratic Party hierarchy, the core of his support came from non-traditional sources, such as labor unions and independent citizens' groups. Further, his position as executive director of the Vermont Forest and Farmland Foundation gave him many useful contacts throughout the state.

Meyer's timing was fortuitous as the Republican candidate, former Governor Harold Arthur, was not a popular figure. Arthur had been the winner in a fractious six-man Republican primary and was reluctant to take stands on key issues. As the campaign wore on,

Arthur's diffidence stood in marked contrast to Meyer's strong views on international affairs and America's standing in the world.

An article in the October 6, 1958 *Bennington Banner* gives a picture of Meyer's appeal as someone outside the conventional political realm. Reporter Phil Savory described Meyer as "displaying an unusual warmth and sincerity in personal conversation.... He is convinced of his beliefs but is not dogmatic in his approach to them." About those beliefs, Savory reported, "He advocates abolishment of a peacetime draft as a waste of money and talent; cessation of the testing and manufacture of atomic and hydrogen bombs; and is critical of the 'rigid' policies of John Foster Dulles," which in Meyer's view were leading our government to support dictators around the world.

Nationally prominent author and social activist Dorothy Canfield Fisher was one of many vocal supporters. Just before Dorothy Canfield Fisher died, in November 1958, she submitted a letter in October to several Vermont newspapers that read, "Let us mark our ballots in favor of the one candidate who has made it clear without any reservations or double-talk that he sees war not only as a tragic hangover from barbarism but as a crime against humanity." Another widely published letter was from Vincent Naramore, later a prominent political pollster but then a St. Michael's College math professor: "Unlike Bill Meyer, Governor Arthur has not had the time to face the people and debate the issues of the day. Can it be that he is hiding away in the tall grass hoping thereby to give the impression that he is a grass roots candidate?"

Meyer actively sought and received endorsements from major daily papers, especially three with the highest circulation in southern Vermont, the *Brattleboro Reformer,* the *Rutland Herald,* and the *Bennington Banner*. In its endorsement, the *Banner* called attention to both Meyer's strengths and the weaknesses of his opponent: "For the first time in many years the Republican Party has failed to come up with the best candidate for the United States Congress....Now the GOP is faced with the deplorable task of defending the inadequacies of Arthur, a task that is becoming a bitter pill....Compared to Arthur, Meyer's campaign has been conducted on a high level. He has stated his beliefs with sincerity and dignity on a number of issues."

Dorothy Canfield Fisher: "Vermont Tradition"

Dorothy Canfield Fisher, a longtime resident of Arlington, Vermont, was an educational reformer, social activist, and best-selling author in the early decades of the twentieth century. An outspoken opponent of McCarthyism, she argued, as here in her book Vermont Tradition *(1953), that there was something basic in the Vermont character that resisted the anti-communist hysteria.*

The Vermont tradition is unwritten, mostly inarticulate, to some degree unconscious and instinctive. Nobody ever places one clause in it above the others. Any one of them will do to begin with. For instance, the unquestioned right of anyone to practice variations—if harmless to others—from the way of life generally accepted by the majority of his neighbors.

Vermonters agree with all other good American citizens that one variation in standards cannot be tolerated because it cannot possibly be considered harmless to others. This exception is obedience to the Communist Party line. Where we Vermonters differ from some American citizens is that in our sincere opposition to communism and our horror at its threats to every liberty dear to us, we try very hard to keep clear in our minds the difference

Dorothy Canfield Fisher, circa 1950
(courtesy of Vermont Historical Society)

between suspicion and proof. In some localities, we note that people usually sensible and wellbalanced have become so worn by longcontinued nervous tension that—so it seems to us—any sort of nonconformity to the average level of popular conduct and belief seems to them sure indication of the wish to destroy our government by force. Not so in Vermont. Just because a young man wears a beard and talks rather foolishly about subjects he obviously does not understand, we do not jump to the conclusion that he must be a secret agent in Moscow.

Teachers naturally have great influence in modeling the opinions of the rising generation. Society is right in demanding from them soundness of mind and character. Unfortunately, in the present wave of fear and suspicion, school boards and citizens committees have often gone to such irrational lengths in demanding proof of loyalty, have insisted on the banning of so many impartial textbooks, that in their history classes only the boldest American teachers dare call attention to the Bill of Rights, which is part of our Constitution.

How about Vermont teachers? Let's turn to the record. Here is a resolution voted by the Champlain Valley Teachers Association at a meeting some years ago, just about at the time when the repressive super-loyalty wave was beginning to sweep over our country:

> WHEREAS, we believe that Democracy is strong enough to stand on its own feet, and defend itself by its tested methods of free research and discussion, weighing freely the merits of all questions by open reasoning rather than by taboos, be it
>
> RESOLVED, that the setting up of a code of orthodox doctrine, and the suppression of all differing modes of thought by some censorship—however well-intended—can only strengthen that spirit of intolerance which in the past has always proved a first step towards dictatorships.

The Teachers Association which passed this resolution was (in Vermont newspapers) neither commended or disapproved. Its members were not called courageous, neither were they labeled subversive. No special notice of any kind was given the resolution. As an expression of American opinion, everybody took it for granted.

Headlines on November 8, 1958, the day after Meyer's historic election (*Bennington Banner* editorial and *Swanton Courier* news story)

"You are the conscience of us all"

When the votes were counted, Republicans had a decline of 22,000 votes from the presidential-year turnout of 1956; the Democratic total only declined by 4,000. It was enough to give Meyer the win, by 3,900 votes. The day after the election, the *Bennington Banner* reported that, finally, Vermont was a two-party state.

The *Swanton Courier* was one of Meyer's most steadfast cheerleaders. Its election story, written by editor-publisher Bernard O'Shea, began with this somewhat convoluted sentence: "Big Bill Meyer, mild, unassuming, quiet, scholarly, who links the problems of Vermont agriculture and forestry which he knows intimately, with the problems of U.S. relations with a hungry, widely destitute world which troubles his conscience and his sense of humanitarian justice, won by 3900 votes over Harold A. Arthur."

In the University of Vermont's William Meyer collection, one can find the following sections: civil rights, civil liberties, conservation, disarmament, economics, clean election, fair trade, the Federal Trade Commission, the Federal Communications Commission, the Federal Power Commission, the Federal Reserve, food stamps, health highways, and housing, among others. Clearly, Meyer was thorough and utterly serious with the responsibilities of his new position. Shortly after arriving in Washington, he became the first Vermont congressman to distribute a newsletter to constituents. By the end of his term, he had been present for 96 percent of the votes.

He gained a seat on the Foreign Affairs Committee and continued to speak out on the issues of war and peace that marked his campaign, urging disarmament (in front of a nearly empty chamber), and voting with a tiny minority against military appropriations. Although his positions on international affairs garnered the headlines, Meyer was especially proud of his legislative advocacy for Vermont farmers, and work against pollution and pesticides. His environmental activism earned him an invitation to join candidate John F. Kennedy's Advisory Committee on Natural Resources.

Karl Meyer recalls that two of his parents' heroes were Supreme Court Justices William O. Douglas and Hugo Black, both strong champions of civil liberties. In fact, the Meyers' file marked "Civil Liberties" is one of the thickest in the UVM collection. File materials

Nearly Empty House Hears Meyer Blast

By VONDA BERGMAN

Burlington Free Press, February 18, 1959

reveal that Meyer followed with interest the case of Willard Uphaus, a theologian whose World Fellowship Center (a self-described "inter-religious, intercultural peace organization") in Albany, New Hampshire, was under attack from that state's right-wing Attorney General, Louis Wyman. Uphaus ultimately served a year in jail for refusing to surrender the membership rolls of the Center. Meyer's intense interest in the case was of concern to his top aides who were fearful of the possibility of guilt-by-association if Meyer spoke out publicly.

But Meyer's feelings about the Red Scare atmosphere were firmly stated in his speech to the Vermont Democratic Convention

---

Congress of the United States
House of Representatives
Washington, D. C.

JUL 16 1960

July 7, 1960

Honorable William H. Meyer
House Office Building
Washington, D. C.

Dear Bill:

Now that Congress has recessed and we have a little breathing spell, I want to thank you sincerely for supporting the recent luncheon on my behalf. The confidence which you have demonstrated in me and your generous financial help have provided much inspiration to me at the beginning of what we know will be an exceedingly difficult campaign.

I have the faith to believe that we are going to win. I appreciate tremendously the contribution you have made toward that success.

Sincerely,

George McGovern

GM/ep

You continue to be the conscience of us all, Bill. Godspeed to you in the 1960 campaign.

Letter from George McGovern to William H. Meyer (courtesy of Karl Meyer)

in May 1960: "I am tired of having my liberties confined because the faint of heart say it must be done to contain communism.... I say to you that this course of action not only could eventually destroy democratic government in the United States, but that it would also lose the global struggle for freedom."

In his one term in office, Meyer found like-minded colleagues on these issues. He worked closely with Robert Kastenmeier of Wisconsin, Edith Green of Oregon, and Byron Johnson of Colorado, among others. Forty of Meyer's colleagues signed an endorsement of Meyer's re-election campaign that ran in several Vermont newspapers, including the *Burlington Free Press*: "We don't know Bill Meyer the campaigner, but we do know Bill Meyer the citizen, and Bill Meyer the Congressman. He has shown a talent for leadership, and a great sense of responsibility. We simply want you to know we view him as a valuable member of Congress." A 1960 letter to Meyer from then congressman George McGovern acknowledged the likelihood of "an exceedingly difficult campaign," adding in a handwritten PS, "You continue to be the conscience of us all, Bill."

"Any good Republican can beat Meyer"

These colleagues no doubt were aware that Meyer would have a much harder battle in 1960, with a Presidential campaign ahead signaling a likely return of Republican voters to the polls. Vermont governor Robert Stafford commented in November 1959, "any good Republican can beat Meyer." By February 1960, Stafford himself, a popular governor and polished campaigner, stepped down from the governor's office to challenge Meyer, confident that "Vermont would dispense with the services of our Democratic Congressman." A headline of May 9, 1960 read, "Meyer Expects GOP To Throw 'Kitchen Sink.'" In that article Meyer observed, "From what I hear, they'll be going after my beliefs and my family."

This was an accurate assessment, as Stafford and other Republicans painted Meyer as having pacifist beliefs, and accused him of being a conscientious objector during World War II. (Actually, he was declared 4-F for medical reasons.) The "family" part of the

'Any Good Republican Can Beat Meyer,' Says Stafford

Morning Press Bureau   'Too Overwhelming'

Burlington Free Press, November 26, 1959

Meyer · Expects GOP To Throw 'Kitchen Sink'

Bennington Banner, May 9, 1960

In North Village

Meyer Lashes Into GOP For "Smear" Campaign

By JONATHAN COTTIN

Bennington Banner, October 13, 1960

Stafford, Meyer Clash In Bitter Debate At Newport

Bennington Banner, October 5, 1960

equation referred to Meyer's son Karl, an activist with the pacifist Catholic Worker movement who had also served jail time for a civil disobedience protest at an Omaha air base.

Bernard O'Shea, publisher of the *Swanton Courier* and Meyer's most trusted political advisor, expressed concern about how Meyer was being portrayed in the press. In a March 1960 personal letter to Meyer, he wrote, "I think (that) on these minority votes on arms questions that you should continue to put out press releases explaining your reasons.... Vermonters should have this military pork barrel explained more closely by their representative, in the public press....My point, Bill, is that we should get on the offensive with this kind of vote and not let these reactions to the minority votes you take put us on the defensive."

During the summer of 1960, the independent citizens' groups that aided Meyer in 1958 were reconstituted and it was soon apparent that establishment Democrats, led by Fred Fayette and Russell Niquette, were not going to actively support Meyer. There was, however, help from an unexpected source: a cadre of Harvard students who were taken with Meyer's candidacy. Meyer's disarmament position caught the attention of Harvard activists in the Committee for a Sane Nuclear Policy (SANE). Todd Gitlin, currently a noted historian and social critic and then a Harvard sophomore, recalls borrowing Harvard professor David Reisman's station wagon to drive with others to Vermont for door-knocking and postering.

Both of Meyer's sons, William Jr. and Karl, recall a campaign that was an uphill struggle. They both recall that their father was not naturally comfortable in the electoral battleground, and thought that simply doing a good job in Washington would warrant re-election. William Jr. said that his father could be blunt, and less than diplomatic. Karl added, "He didn't win friends when he got moralistic with the machine Democrats." This is also the recollection of Peter Jacobson, a summer volunteer from the University of Chicago who ultimately got close to the inner circle: "I was convinced that if I could get him to play a little friendly ball with the politicos he so deprecated and disdained, we would carry the day."

Meyer sensed he was about to lose the endorsements of newspapers that supported him in 1958. His response was an eight-page document, "The Meyer Record," distributed throughout the state, with articles designed to solidify and broaden his support. Some of the headlines demonstrate that Meyer did not simply want to be known for his provocative stands on foreign policy: "Wildlife Federation Hails Meyer's Work," "Meyer Lauds Rural Electrification on Anniversary," "Meyer School Milk Bill Benefits Many." An introductory piece on the front page, however, alerted readers to what Meyer believed what was at stake. He headlined his piece: "Voters see the opposition's vague allusions to 'patriotism' and 'Americanism' as clumsy attempts to hide Meyer's outstanding record in Congress."

An aggressive Stafford challenged Meyer's foreign policy positions in the first of several debates that fall. Meyer defended his stance on recognition of China: "Let's oppose them all the way, but get them in a place (the United Nations) where we can subject them to world opinion." As the Associated Press reported, "Meyer said that everyone knows that the admission of the Chinese communists to the UN will be an eventual reality and that the United States is losing bargaining power on the issue."

But an incident in the second debate may have slowed whatever momentum Meyer was gaining. It started with a letter to several Vermont newspapers from Vrest Orton, founder of Weston's Country Store and a Stafford supporter. The letter called Meyer soft on communism and added, "Bob Stafford believes in and practices the ideals and moral precepts of the Christian religion. Since Meyer, by his record favors those (communists) who do not, what religion does Meyer profess and what church does he belong to?" During the debate, sponsored by the Burlington League of Women Voters, Stafford denied any connection with the letter, and Meyer, losing his temper, challenged the governor to take a lie-detector test on live television. The *Springfield Reporter* called this exchange a "blatant outburst of boorishness" and further editorialized, "Vermonters don't like to see conduct like this on a speaker's platform."

No newspaper questioned Meyer's integrity, just whether he was foolish or misguided or representative of Vermont's population.

The *Bennington Banner,* one of the major newspapers that supported Meyer two years earlier, this time endorsed Stafford. "Either Mr. Meyer is a pacifist or he is an idealist and in our opinion he is both....We believe that he is dedicated to his own personal idealistic beliefs which often run counter to popular thinking."

It might be tempting to blame Meyer's defeat that November on "Red-baiting" and resistance to his progressive politics, but the numbers tell a different story. Meyer actually got 7,000 more votes than he had in 1958. However, the presidential contest increased the turnout significantly, with Richard Nixon winning 58 percent of the Vermont vote. The enormous upsurge of Republican voters (43,000 more than in 1958) sealed Meyer's fate. Even if he had garnered the full support of the Democratic establishment, it is unlikely he would have prevailed.

In 1962, Vermont took another major step towards becoming a two-party state with the first of Philip Hoff's victories in the governor's race. But Meyer's day as a Democratic star had passed. He was an unsuccessful Democratic candidate for the U.S. Senate in 1962, 1964, and 1968. Alarmed at the support of many Democrats for the Vietnam War, he and a small group (including recent Vermont transplant Bernie Sanders) founded the left-leaning, anti-war Liberty Union Party in 1970.

Martha Abbott attended the founding meeting of the Liberty Union as a University of Vermont student. "Bill was totally respectful, despite my youth," she recalls. "He was warmly supportive and encouraged me to get involved." Meyer was the Liberty Union's candidate for Senate in 1970 and for the House in 1972, remaining active in local politics until his death in 1983.

Meyer's old colleague Bernard O'Shea lamented his passing in a *Burlington Free Press* obituary: "He was a man who wanted to represent the electorate and challenge them at the same time. He had a vision of what he wanted to have happen, and much of what he wanted came to pass."

Sinclair Lewis' 1935 novel was adapted for the stage, and produced by the Federal Theatre Project (By Works Progress Administration [Public domain], via Wikimedia Commons)

Afterword

I first formed my mental picture of Vermont in the early 1960s, as a result of reading Sinclair Lewis' *It Can't Happen Here,* written in 1935. I was a suburban teenager and it was yet another ten years before I actually set foot in the state that has been my home now for over forty years. The book gave me an idea of rural life and the "Yankee" principles that Lewis' hero, Doremus Jessup, embodied. Jessup is a newspaper editor who sees something dark brewing in American politics: a potential for a Fascist dictatorship. The bravery of Jessup in resisting authoritarianism was inspiring to me— and I thought once more about his qualities while researching this book, especially as I read the editorials of John Drysdale (the *White River Valley Herald*), Robert Mitchell (the *Rutland Herald*), Bernard O'Shea (the *Swanton Courier*), and others.

Lewis, who spent a good part of each year in Barnard, Vermont, had an appreciation of Vermont's small-town values, but also feared that, given the right circumstances, conformity and authoritarianism would threaten a sense of community-held principles. The events covered in this book are not as dramatic as Lewis' scenario, which concludes with Jessup joining a resistance force in Minnesota. The authors of *Freedom and Unity,* a 2004 Vermont history by Jeff Potash, Michael Sherman, and Gene Sessions, acknowledge that Vermont escaped the worst aspects of the Red Scare, but they also note that "the perceived Vermont virtues [of individual liberties and communal trust] extolled by writers and commentators were severely tested."

This book concludes with William H. Meyer's loss in the 1960 Congressional election, in part because of his call for admission of "Red China" to the United Nations and his plea for nuclear disarmament. Just two years later, Vermont truly became a two-party state with the election of Democrat Phil Hoff for the first of his three innovative terms. In the years since then, Vermont's national profile has been transformed: there has been the back-to-the-land movement, the unconventional career of Bernie Sanders, the nuclear freeze campaign, the environmental movement, the first civil union law in the country, Howard Dean's presidential run of 2004, and our current (as of 2018) congressional delega-

Bernie Sanders, attacked as a "socialist fungus," ushers in a new political era as he wins election as Burlington's mayor in 1980. (courtesy of Rob Swanson)

tion's strong opposition to the Iraq War and more recently, to the policies of reactionary Republicans.

But it has not all been a drift to the left. Just ask political activist and scholar Michael Parenti, who was fired for his views in 1971 by the University of Vermont's Board of Trustees. Bernie Sanders was often red-baited; Democrat Joyce Desautels of Burlington's Board of Aldermen, called him a "socialist fungus" and accused him of trying to expand the Socialist Party base in Burlington. Sanders opponents over the years have tried and failed to tar him with his professed support of "democratic Socialism" or for the Cuban Revolution. Nativism and distrust of the outsider occasionally rise to the surface, as it did in 2000 with the "Take Back Vermont" movement in opposition to civil unions for same-sex couples.

Richard Hathaway wrote in 1988 that "we have yet to comprehend fully the legacy of McCarthy and McCarthyism." That statement is still true thirty years later. The definitive history of this era in Vermont is still to be written; I have described nine episodes that illustrate the range of principled opposition, timid acquiescence, and strident demagoguery. Across the nation, at the current moment, we are witnessing a resurgence of the forces that, in 1950, Senator Margaret Chase Smith of Maine called the "Four Horsemen of Calumny: Fear, Ignorance, Bigotry, and Smear." Vermont may be tested once again.

– Rick Winston

Sources

In early 1988, I volunteered to be the researcher for the conference "Vermont in the McCarthy Era." This introduced me to the joys (and also the neck pain and eye strain) of working with the microfiche machines in the Vermont State Library. It was thrilling to feel propelled back into another era through its daily newspapers and illuminating to see how historical events of the Cold War such as the Indochina conflict, the execution of Julius and Ethel Rosenberg, and coups in Guatemala and Iran were covered in local papers. It turned out that I also needed a measure of focus not to get distracted by the World Series news or the features at the local movie houses (my favorite was a St. Albans double bill of a Roy Rogers western with "I Was a Communist for the F.B.I.")

If anyone is inspired to do some more reading about these times, here is a list of the sources that I used.

Comprehensive Histories of the Red Scare Era:

A list of books on this period and its personalities would fill several pages. I'll just mention some that were most helpful to me. Ellen Schrecker, who was a speaker at our 1988 conference, has written several books on the subject. Two are *Many Are the Crimes* (Princeton University Press, 1998) and *No Ivory Tower* (Oxford University Press, 1986). Marjorie Heins' *Priests of Our Democracy: The Supreme Court, Academic Freedom, and the Anti-Communist Purge* (New York University Press, 2013), Richard M. Fried's *Nightmare in Red*

(Oxford University Press, 1990), David Oshinsky's *A Conspiracy So Immense* (Oxford University Press, 2005), and Victor Navasky's *Naming Names* (Viking Press, 1980) are some of the many others.

Chapter One:
The Congressman and the Professor

Just as I started writing this chapter, I learned that my neighbor Andrew S. Nuquist had just donated his father's scrapbook of the 1946 campaign to the University of Vermont Special Collection. It became an invaluable resource for me. Charles Plumley kept two scrapbooks: one is available at the Vermont History Center in Barre, the other at the Norwich University Library. Newspapers of the time, especially the *Suburban List* (available in bound copies in the Brownell Library in Essex Junction, Vermont), the *Bennington Banner,* and the *Barre Daily Times* filled in a lot of the gaps. Andrew E. Nuquist's daughter, Elizabeth Raby, reminisced about the campaign in the 2002 Summer/Fall issue of *Vermont History,* also published as a chapter in her memoir *Ransomed Voices* (Red Mountain Press, 2013).

Chapter Two:
The Henry Wallace Campaign in Vermont

For an overview on Wallace, I found John Culver and John Hyde's *American Dreamer: The Life of Henry Wallace* (W.W. Norton, 2001) very insightful. For in-depth coverage on the historic 1948 campaign, there is Curtis MacDougall's *Gideon's Army,* (Marzani and Munsell, 1952) which offers a state-by-state rundown on the campaign. Alex Ross' article for the *New Yorker,* "Uncommon Man," (October 14, 2013) explores Wallace perplexing and contradictory personality. James Hayford's memoir *Recollecting Who I Was* (Oriole Books, 2003) has a first-hand view of the Wallace campaign in Vermont. The coverage of the Vermont campaign in the *Burlington Daily News* and the *Burlington Free Press* provided the core of this chapter.

Chapter Three:
A Sinister Poison: The 'Red Scare' Comes to Bethel

The 1950 controversy involving Vilhjalmur Stefansson and Owen Lattimore was not featured in the 1988 conference, although an article from the *Burlington Free Press* about the event was reprinted in the conference booklet. It was when I followed this thread that I had an experience that I'm sure every researcher dreams about: when I met M. Dickey Drysdale, the publisher and editor of *The Herald of Randolph* at his office and explained my project, he went to a shelf and pulled down a folder of his father's labeled "Red Scare Bethel;" it contained every news story and editorial that his father had written. As is related in the chapter, the story quickly became too big for a weekly, and Drysdale called on his colleagues Robert Mitchell (the *Rutland Herald*) and John Hooper (the *Brattleboro Reformer*) to follow up. The controversy was confined to late July and mid-August of 1950, so those three newspapers provide a wealth of material. Books that were especially helpful were Stefansson's *Discovery,* (McGraw-Hill Book Company, 1964) Evelyn Stefansson Nef's *Finding My Way,* (The Francis Press, 2002) and Robert Newman's *Owen Lattimore and the "Loss" of China* (University of California Press, 1991).

Chapter Four:
Defending Alex Novikoff; the Legacy of Arnold Schein

David Holmes' 1991 book on the Novikoff case, *Stalking the Academic Communist* (University Press of New England) is essential reading for understanding all aspects of this controversy. Holmes and Arnold Schein both were speakers at the 1988 conference, and their comments can be heard at the Vermont History Center in Barre. Mark Greenberg interviewed both Schein and one of Novikoff's other passionate defenders, Rabbi Max Wall (as well as the University of Vermont's attorney Louis Lisman), for the *Green Mountain Chronicles* radio program, sponsored by the Vermont Historical Society. The case made headlines through the spring and summer of 1953, and it is fascinating to watch the case unfold through the pages of the *Burlington Free Press* and *Burlington Daily News*. Both papers supported Novikoff's firing, so it is especially refreshing to read several editorials by Bernard O'Shea of the *Swanton Courier* in Novikoff's defense. I'm grateful to Susan Schein of Burlington for sharing memories of her father and some of her father's writings on the case.

Chapter Five:
From "Peiping" to Putney; the Hinton Family and the Red Scare

Susan McIntyre Lloyd's book, *The Putney School: A Progressive Experiment* (Yale University Press, 1987), is a fascinating history of the Hinton family and an influential educational institution. The archives at Putney School houses all of her notes, which were very helpful. The British journalist Gerry Kennedy discovered that he was related to the Hinton family and wrote a history, *The Booles and the Hintons* (Cork University Press, 2016); he was able to interview Joan Hinton at length before her death in 2011. I was surprised by the paucity of local coverage of William Hinton's testimony before the Senate Internal Security Committee in July 1954. I was able to get more information from both *Time Magazine* and the *New York Times*.

Chapter Six:
The Vermont Press and Joseph McCarthy's Downfall

There was certainly no lack of Vermont coverage when Senator Ralph Flanders issued a series of challenges to the power of Senator McCarthy. Flanders was often on the front page of the *Rutland Herald* from the spring of 1954 through that fall, and publisher/editor Robert Mitchell was one his most vocal defenders. Some of the editorials are featured in Tyler Resch's book *The Bob Mitchell Years*. (*Rutland Herald,* 1994) Mitchell was not alone, and it was intriguing to see very forthright anti-McCarthy editorials in the *Springfield Reporter* and *Swanton Courier,* among others. As usual, the *Burlington Daily News* provided the pro-McCarthy and anti-Flanders slant. Ralph Flanders also devoted a chapter to the censure movement in his memoir, *Senator from Vermont* (Little, Brown, 1961).

Chapter Seven:
Bernard O'Shea and the *Swanton Courier*

In 1985, Bernard ("Bun") O'Shea presented the Swanton Historical Society with a complete run of the *Swanton Couriers,* from 1949 until the paper's relocation to Enosburg Falls. After hours of craning my neck in the Vermont State Library, it was a pleasure to sit at a quiet desk in Swanton and actually turn pages of the *Courier.* Most of the material in this chapter comes from that session. I also had conversations with Nat and Nini Worman, Roy Towlen, Robin Lloyd, Tyrone Shaw, Chris O'Shea, Kevin O'Shea, and Richard Cowperthwaite about their memories of Bun.

Chapter Eight:
Meanwhile, Across the Connecticut River...

The recording of Paul Sweezy's recollections of his persecution in New Hampshire is at the Vermont History Center in Barre. An article in the University of New Hampshire alumni magazine, "Courage Under Fire" (October 2001), pays tribute to Gwynne Harris Daggett and details his troubles with Attorney General Wyman's investigation. The Daggett and Sweezy cases are also covered in *New Hampshire's University* by Everett Sackett (New Hampshire Publishing, 1974). Willard Uphaus wrote a moving memoir, *Commitment* (McGraw-Hill, 1963) about the same period of time. There is also an extensive file labeled "Uphaus" in William H. Meyer's papers at the University of Vermont Special Collections. The full exchange between John McClaughry and Michael Sherman is in the Vermont Historical Society archives.

Chapter Nine:
The Congressional Campaigns of William H. Meyer

William Meyer's hometown paper was the *Bennington Banner,* and it is instructive to follow Meyer's fortunes through its pages. Meyer's election in 1958 and the hard-fought re-election campaign were covered at length in most Vermont newspapers. In 1962, Peter Jacobson and Earl Medzinsky wrote an exhaustive article dissecting both campaigns for *New University Thought,* a publication of the University of Chicago (in the Vermont Historical Society collection). I had lengthy conversations with both Meyer's sons, William Jr. and Karl. Karl provided me with a copy of "The Meyer Record," an eight-page document distributed during the 1960 campaign.

Acknowledgments

This book owes its publication to Stephen McArthur of Rootstock Publishing, who believed in its timeliness and its value for Vermont and elsewhere. I was fortunate to have an editorial team of the first order: editor Jim Higgins, copy editors Laurie Lieb and Mark Greenberg, and designer Mason Singer of Laughing Bear Associates.

Academics often have a reputation for being unwelcoming to lay historians, but I've had nothing but encouragement from some of Vermont's finest historians: Tyler Resch, Gregory Sanford, and Charles Morrissey. Thanks especially must go to Michael Sherman; we worked together on the 1988 conference "Vermont in the McCarthy Era," and since then he has been an enthusiastic supporter of my efforts to make this story known.

Thanks to my fellow "community historian" Paul Heller for advice and for loaning me the title of this book.

Thanks to the librarians who helped me with my research: Ilana Grallert of the Rauner Library at Dartmouth College, Paul Carnahan and Marjorie Strong at the Leahy Library of the Vermont History Center, Prudence Doherty at the University of Vermont's Bailey-Howe Library Special Collections, Randy Smith at the Putney School, Tom McMurdo and Mara Siegel at the Vermont State

Library, and the staff at the Vermont State Archives in Middlesex. Thanks also to Ronald Kilburn of the Swanton Historical Society, and to Mark Greenberg for providing transcripts of interviews with Kendall Wild, Arnold Schein and Max Wall.

I was too late to talk to many of the principal actors in this book, but was fortunate to make the acquaintance of the next generation, who shared memories of their parents. Thanks to Susan Schein, Richard Macnair, Marni Rosner, M. Dickey Drysdale, William Meyer Jr. and Karl Meyer, Martha Sweezy, Andrew S. Nuquist, the O'Shea clan (Kevin, Chris, Ross, Ellen, and Clare), and Priscilla Daggett.

Thanks also to Susan Ritz, Andy Christiansen, Susan Lloyd, Joseph Gainza, Allen Gilbert, Joe Sherman, Bill Schubart, Peter Jacobson, Steve Early, Howard Norman, Karen Lane, Tim Calabro, Kate Mueller, Ellen David-Friedman, and Marjorie Heins.

Finally, it's hard to overstate the contributions of my wife Andrea Serota at every step of the long and often circuitous process that resulted in this book. She was a first reader, pronoun wrangler, fount of insightful advice, critical questioner, and morale booster.

A note regarding the graphics: The newspaper clippings have been gleaned from a variety of often less than ideal sources. Many have been scanned from old photocopies or from faded and yellowed newspapers. Every effort has been made to clean them up for reproduction while staying true to their current condition. Their visual clarity may not be ideal but their historic value is important as a reflection of the time.

Index

Jeb Wallace-Brodeur

RICK WINSTON grew up in Yonkers, New York, and attended both Columbia University and University of California, Berkeley. He arrived in Adamant, Vermont in 1970, and still lives there. He started Montpelier's Lightning Ridge Film Society in 1972. That became the Savoy Theater in 1981, which soon established Montpelier as a mecca for lovers of foreign, independent, and generally off-beat films. He is currently teaching film history in several places, including Community College of Vermont. His long-standing interest in the Red Scare era led him to become one of the organizers of the 1988 Montpelier conference, "Vermont in the McCarthy Era."

CPSIA information can be obtained
at www.ICGtesting.com
Printed in the USA
LVHW05s0854270718
584953LV00007B/14/P